ISBN: 9781290641029

Published by:
HardPress Publishing
8345 NW 66TH ST #2561
MIAMI FL 33166-2626

Email: info@hardpress.net
Web: http://www.hardpress.net

Presented to the
LIBRARY *of the*
UNIVERSITY OF TORONTO
from
the estate of
MARK SELTZER

Each in his narrow cell for ever laid
The rude forefathers of the hamlet sleep.
                              GRAY, *Elegy*, v. 4.

EPITAPHS:

QUAINT, CURIOUS, AND ELEGANT.

WITH REMARKS ON THE

Obsequies of Various Nations.

COMPILED AND COLLATED BY

HENRY JAMES LOARING,

AUTHOR OF "COMMON SAYINGS, WORDS AND CUSTOMS," ETC.

LONDON: WILLIAM TEGG

PREFACE.

EPITAPHS form a connecting link between the past, the present, and the future.

Under the greatest bodily sufferings man still feels the endearing tie of life, and is solicitous not to be forgotten, and he who preserves a monument, records a name, or rescues an inscription that is nearly effaced, is entitled to remembrance.

This Collection is the result of personal observation, research, and friendly contributions, during the last twenty years.

Epitaphs in Churches and Churchyards, generally speaking, belong to one of the following classes:

(1) *Elegant*, (2) *Trade and Professional*, (3) *Witty and Grotesque*. The compiler has therefore placed them in chapters under those heads. The remainder, which there is some difficulty in classifying, it has been found advisable to introduce at the end as *Miscellaneous*.

CONTENTS.

	PAGE
INTRODUCTORY	1
ELEGANT EPITAPHS	22
PROFESSIONAL EPITAPHS	85
WITTY AND GROTESQUE	144
MISCELLANEOUS EPITAPHS	201

INTRODUCTORY.

EPITAPHS doubtless originated in a sense of immortality. Their invention is attributed to the scholars of Linus, the Theban poet, who flourished about the 2,700th year of the world, and being unhappily slain, his scholars lamented the loss of their master in a particular kind of mournful verses, called from him Ælinum, and afterwards Epitaphia, because they were sung at burials, and engraved upon sepulchres, which may be called Monuments *à Memoria*, as they were memorials to put men in mind of the instability of human nature, and the loss of their departed friends, as also to excite their meditation by the ideas of death, to a reformation of life.

Monuments and inscriptions form the cementing link between the past, the present, and the future. They may be considered in another view, as tributes of surviving relatives and friends who labour to preserve a name from oblivion; this is a wish natural to the human heart, a desire congenial to the best and purest of our species. Under the greatest bodily sufferings, man still feels the endearing tie of life, and is solicitous not to be forgotten, and he who preserves a monument from mouldering into ruin, who records a name, or rescues an inscription that is nearly effaced, encourages a useful propensity, the universal passion, and he is entitled in his turn not to be overlooked as a trifler, or as a labourer who has busied himself about nothing. Epitaphs are of extensive use in tracing descents and pedigrees, as well as in ascertaining the time when the party deceased. And it is certainly most desirable that some plan should be adopted for preserving monumental inscriptions from the influence of time and chance.

Epitaphs were used by the ancient Jews, and most of the nations of antiquity. The Athenians placed a kind of scroll over the burying places of their dead, with the name inscribed, and an expression of their good wishes thereon. The Lacedemonians would only allow epitaphs to those who died honourably in battle. The Greeks, even in the earliest times, were wont to inscribe the monumental columns which they raised in memory of the dead, with appropriate legends—generally in verse—briefly celebrating the virtues and distinctions of the deceased. The Spartans, with their stern disdain of conventionalities, and abhorrence of social affections, interdicted epitaphs, except upon the tombs of warriors, and matrons who died in travail. The Romans inscribed epitaphs to the spirits of the departed, and ancient tombs still exist in the roads near Rome, from which the words so frequently seen in modern epitaphs are derived, namely, "*Siste Viator*"— "Stop traveller." Turning to the French, we find that epitaphs were at one time elevated into an aristocratic privilege, and reserved for the especial delectation of lords and gentlemen.

"Earth to earth," and "Dust to dust" seems to have been the undeviating custom of primeval man. Adam, according to Persian tradition, was buried in the island of Serendib, and mighty lions for a long period guarded the burial spot. The resting places of the first glorious women of the world, are still pointed out to the traveller in the Holy Land,—Eve and Sarah, Rebecca and Leah, sleep their last sleep, all quiet in the dust. Nor was it till later ages that any other custom prevailed, and that imported from a foreign land. Israel, the first of the great patriarchate, who, by his son Joseph, was swathed in cerecloths, and embalmed, was placed in one of the huge coffins of Egypt.

The following passage in Herodotus leads us to suppose that the Ethiopians placed their dead in glass coffins: "Let us next consider their sepulchres, which are said to be constructed of glass. When dead, they dry the body, cover it completely with plaster, and exhibit it ornamented with pictures resembling the deceased. They then dig a grave, and cover it with glass, through which the body is visible, neither emitting a disagreeable smell, nor showing any signs of corruption."

Thucydides, speaking of the manner in which Ethiopians dispose of their dead, says, in the third book of his history: "Some throw them into the river; others preserve them in their houses, after having inclosed them, as it were, in a coffin of glass." In another passage the same author says: "The Ethiopians conduct the funerals of their dead in a very singular manner. The body is first salted to keep it from putrefaction, and then placed in a grave covered with glass, that it may be seen through," as we read in Herodotus. But Clefias Cnidius denies this, telling us that the bodies are indeed salted, but never inclosed in glass; for the likeness of the dead could not in that way be retained, as the body would first become shrivelled and parched, and then totally decay. A hollow statue of gold is therefore cast to contain the body, and this being placed in some conspicuous situation, and covered with glass, it may be said that a similitude is exhibited through glass. It is in this manner the funerals of the rich are solemnized, while persons of smaller fortune are deposited in statues of silver, and the poor in baked clay. Glass is common to all, Ethiopia producing it in such abundance that it is found everywhere by the inhabitants.

Egypt excelled all other lands in the splendour of her tombs; the Libyan and Arabian mountains are strewn with them, and the pyramids are the monuments of kings.

Cromlechs were burial places, and abound in England, Ireland, Scotland, in the heart of India, and many other parts of the known world. These cromlechs, when in a perfect state, consist of three or more stones, unhewn, and are generally so placed as to form a small enclosure, over these a large stone is laid, the whole forming a kind of rude chamber.

The remains of crosses are interesting, as the common sign of the Christian faith, beneath which our converted ancestors performed divine worship previously to the erection of churches. They were usually set up in cross ways, or in the most frequented part of any town. Some of these were probably removed afterwards into churchyards, and new ones erected in conspicuous situations, for the purpose, as it is supposed, of putting the passers-by in mind of offering up their prayers for the dead, whose remains were therein deposited.

Burning the bodies of the dead had probably its origin

in the endeavour to prevent any insult or ill-treatment being offered them. When a wealthy Egyptian died, his body was removed, and embalmed by his physicians, who appear to have united the profession of a surgeon with the business of a barber. The process of embalming was both tedious and expensive; occupying seventy days in the performance. In ancient Greece, the bodies of the dead were consumed by fire. The Athenians occasionally interred their bodies in the earth, but it appears that by law the practice of burning was enjoined.

The practice of burning the dead among the ancient Romans was attended with numerous and pompous ceremonies, and existed from a remote period. The deceased remained for seven days unburied, and on each day was washed with hot water and fragrant oils, that in case he only slumbered, he might thus be awakened.

The funeral of Cornelius Sylla, the celebrated dictator, was very splendid; the body was attended by the whole of the Senate and the Vestal Virgins, and hymns were chanted in celebration of his great achievements. When the Emperor Tiberius died, his corpse was buried in Rome with much pomp, and his successor, Caligula, pronounced his funeral oration.

The Chaldeans—otherwise known as the Babylonians —were worshippers of the igneous principle. This people deeming it a sacrilege to the sun to consume the dead by fire, they accordingly embalmed the bodies in honey, and so preserved them. Their funeral ceremonies and lamentations greatly resembled the Egyptians.

The Bactrians, who were the inhabitants of an ancient kingdom of Asia, now called Khorassan, not only suffered the corpses of their friends and relatives to be eaten by dogs, but, it is said, kept large and savage ones to devour such as lived to an extreme age, or were enfeebled and useless through long sickness.

The Ichthyophagi, or fish-eaters—a people mentioned by Ptolemy, and inhabiting the region which lay between Carmania and Gedrosia, bordering on the Persian Gulf—invariably committed their dead to the sea; and by this means they repaid in the completest manner the obligations which they had incurred to its inhabitants. They constructed their huts of large fish-bones, of which the ribs of the whale served them for beams and rafters, and the jaws for doors. The mortars in which they pounded their fish—the vessels wherein they set it to bake in the sun—and the bowls which formed their dishes at table, were nothing else than the joints of the vertebræ of the same sea-monster.

The Scythians had a mode of disposing of their dead, peculiarly their own. They objected to burial in the earth, drowning in the sea, and destruction by fire; and having thus rejected three of the elements, made choice of the fourth—and suspended the bodies in the air. Ælian records that the dead were sewn up first in skins, for fear that birds of prey should devour them; they were then suspended on the branches of trees, and so gradually decayed, the sport of every breath and every storm.

The Colchians hung up this strange fruit among the foliage of their native forests.

The Heruli women hung themselves, on the death of their husbands—not from an impulse of any great affection, but because it was fashionable to do so; and their neighbours, by avoiding their society, would have punished the breach of propriety they committed in venturing to live. In another district of Scythia, the lamenting friends and weeping relatives of the departed testified the depth of their grief and the height of their affection by eating him—the extent of their love being gauged by the extent of their appetite.

The Balearians, who inhabited the islands now known by the names of Majorca and Minorca, had a still more revolting custom of inhumation; they bruised the flesh and broke the bones of the corpse, crammed them into urns, and laid heaps of wood upon them.

The mode of sepulture employed by the ancient Britons is involved in much obscurity. When the grave of Prince Arthur, in the Abbey of Glastonbury, was opened by command of Henry II., Giraldus Cambriensis, who was present, beheld the bones of that monarch lying in the trunk of a tree, with his sword on one side of him, and his beautiful queen Gueniver on the other.

In England, tombstones were introduced at an early period, and no attempt was ever made to confine them to any particular class. It also appears they were in use subsequent to the introduction of Christianity, as we read in the Old Testament that people were buried in caves, under trees, and in other convenient places; but the custom of burying the dead in enclosed grounds expressly set apart for that purpose, was not established before the year 200.

Any person may now erect a monument in any church or churchyard, so that it does not hinder the celebration of divine worship, and the defacing of it is punishable at common law.

In the year 590, Pope Gregory authorized the relatives of the deceased to erect tablets to their memory, that on reading the inscription they might be induced to offer up prayers for the welfare of their souls; nor did church-yards become common till the latter end of the seventh century.

The pomp of funerals is strictly the heraldic array of a baronial burial. The two men, mutes, who stand at the doors, being supposed to be the two porters of the castle, with their staves in black; the man who heads the procession, wearing a scarf, being a representative of a herald-at-arms; the man who carries a plume of feathers on his head being an esquire, who bears the shield and casque, with its plume (of feathers); the pall-bearers, with batons, being representatives of knights-companions-at-arms; the men walking with wands being supposed to represent gentlemen ushers with their wands. Literally, all the pomp and circumstance with which the barons of high birth, ancient lineage, numerous heraldic quarterings, and large estates, were conveyed in olden times to "the house appointed unto all living," are now copied without the slightest significance or utility, the mere dry form transplanted into another grade and class, to which it is singularly inappropriate, and oppressively expensive.

Wearing mourning must have been a very ancient custom, as Abraham mourned for Sarah, Isaac for his father, and the children of Israel for Moses. But on the death of a friend, it is customary in most European countries to wear black, this colour being deemed the most solemn. This is not so, however, for there are many more beautiful expressions of condolence. In Eastern Asia and other parts, different colours are preferred; for instance, the Chinese, Romans, and Spartans wore white, emblematical of their friends being in Paradise, clad in robes of pure white; and the law ordained a twelve-months' mourning for a husband only. The Egyptians wear yellow, in allusion to the fall and decay of the leaf. The Ethiopians, adopt brown, implying that the body has returned to its native brown earth. The Turks wear violet, in allusion to the early spring flower, or hope on one side, and sorrow on the other. The kings of France also wear violet; our kings, as kings of France, used to do the same, but the sovereign of England mourns in purple. The Islanders of the Pacific wear grey, thereby implying that grey hairs go down to the grave in sorrow.

The Egyptian women went weekly to pray and weep at the sepulchres of the dead, and it is their custom to scatter a peculiar kind of herb thereon. In Turkey and Asia Minor, they adorn the graves with leaves of the palm tree, boughs of myrtle and cypress, placed at the head and foot. At Aleppo, they cultivate myrtles, because they continue green a long period. Yew trees are common in our churchyards on account of their being ever green, and furnishing branches for the decoration of churches. They are more ancient than the conversion of the Saxons, and from the number which still remain it seems probable that they were generally planted as a necessary part of the grave's furniture. At times we see four, one at each corner of the churchyard, but more commonly there is only one, and that usually on the south side. Every one has seen burying places of all conceivable kinds, and every one knows how prominent a feature they form in the English landscape. The Germans call a churchyard the garden of God.

It was in former times the practice to plant herbs and flowers about the grave, and it is still a mark of pure affection, as may be seen by a visit to our cemeteries ; but in other parts of the world it is more prevalent than in England.

The widow's cap intimates that the wife, being one with her husband, has, in a manner, died with him.

How sublime was that most beautiful custom of the ancients, who buried the young at morning twilight; for as they strove to give the softest interpretation to death, so they imagined that "Aurora," the goddess of the morning, who loved the young, had stolen them to her embrace !

The Russians are highly superstitious about the dead. On the day the funeral takes place, the body is accompanied to the grave with many outward testimonies of grief by the relations ; the priest then produces a paper, drawn up and signed by the bishop and another clergyman, which purports to be the passport that will admit the deceased to heaven. The precious document is placed between the fingers of the corpse, and the sorrowing friends having seen the earth closed over him, return to the house of the departed, where they indulge in affliction and brandy for forty days.

There is no business in the life of a Chinese so important to him as his funeral, and no object of art or science in which he is so much interested as his coffin. A wealthy man will expend 1,000 crowns upon this ghastly piece of vanity ; a poor man will give all he is worth ; and a son is frequently known to sell himself for a slave, that he may purchase a rich coffin for his father.

The Burmese practise the rites of cremation, and attach great importance to the ceremonies of their funerals. When a man of rank dies, his body is enclosed in a varnished coffin, and the *talapoins*, or priests, sing solemn hymns over it. After a grand procession, the body is laid upon a pyre of precious woods, erected near some temple; and the spectacle is frequently heightened in magnificence by the introduction of theatrical performances. After the pyre has been lighted, it is suffered to burn till a considerable part of it is consumed, when the body is rescued from the flames, and the remaining portion interred in the neighbouring cemetery.

The Tonquinese burn the bodies, and deposit the ashes in cinerary urns.

The funeral ceremonies of Turkey are particularly solemn and well ordered. The body is carried by the nearest relations of the deceased, chanting passages from the Koran, and by them deposited in a mosque. From thence it is again carried to the cemetery, and buried by the *imaum*, or priest, who pronounces over it a funeral sermon.

When a native of Guinea expires, his wives and relations commence howling hideously, and proceed to shave their heads, and smear a chalky substance over their bodies, as outward tokens of their despair. The body is dressed in its best attire, with its most valuable coral ornaments, scimitar, and other articles of personal adornment, and laid in a coffin, with its fetiches beside it.

The Congoese kindle fires all round the body, at a sufficient distance to preserve it from ignition; and as fast as the clothes absorb the moisture, they renew them, till the body is completely dried. It is is then buried with great pomp.

A Hottentot is taken to some cave or cleft in a neighbouring rock, and there left; but they are careful to close up the entrance with stones, that the body may escape being devoured by wild beasts.

In Otaheite, some of the hair is plucked from the head of the corpse, and the left eye taken out, after which the body is buried.

The American Indians practise several different modes of burial, and some tribes have been known to burn the bodies of their dead warriors.

The tribes of Oonalaska and Nootka Sound inter their dead on the tops of hills, and place a little tumulus over the grave. Every passer-by throws a stone on the heap, which soon becomes of a large size.

The funeral of a Circassian is attended with the most solemn sacrifices to their church, which is a corruption of Christianity.

The funeral of a Georgian occasions great expense to his family, in consequence of the extreme rapacity of the clergy, who then receive enormous fees from the dead as well as the living.

On the death of a relation, the Mingrelians give way to violent expressions of grief, which, on the day of interment, they contrive to drown in intoxication.

The Tartar tribes practise both cremation and burial. The Mongol Tartars burn the bodies of their princes and chief-priests.

The deceased Laplander is wrapt in woollen or linen coverings, and laid in the coffin by some person selected for that service, who is protected against the ill-will of the manes by a consecrated brass ring attached to his left arm.

The frightful custom which formerly prevailed, whenever a Hindoo left a widow at his death, of the unfortunate woman offering herself alive on the funeral pile of her husband, is now almost abandoned.

At Middleburg, in the Netherlands, a singular custom was formerly observed. When any inhabitant died, a bundle of straw was placed before the house, with the ears toward the street, if the deceased was a man, but toward the house, if a woman.

There is, or was a few years since, a peculiar custom in use at Hexham, in the county of Northumberland; namely, an invitation to a burial proclaimed through the public bellman to the inhabitants, and in the subjoined terms: " Blessed are the dead which die in the Lord; Colin James is departed, son of Henry James, who was. Their company is desired to-morrow at three o'clock, and at four he is to be bu—ri—ed. For him and all faithful people give God most hearty thanks."

At Hatherleigh, in Devonshire, after a funeral, the church bells ring a lively peal, as in other places after a wedding; and to this custom the parishioners are perfectly reconciled by the consideration that the deceased is removed from a scene of trouble to a state of peace.

The custom of howling at funerals originated with the Irish, who, in the present day, make a great outcry on the decease of their friends, hoping thus to awaken the soul, which they suppose might otherwise be inactive. It was, however, practised by the Greeks, Arabs, and Romans; the latter had their *præficæ*, whose duty it was to superintend the manner and form of the lamentation.

It is usual in the south of France to erect in the churchyard a lofty pillar, bearing a large lamp, which throws its light upon the cemetery during the night. The custom began at a very early period, between the twelfth and thirteenth century. Sometimes the *lanterne des morts*—death lantern—was a highly ornamental chapel, built in a circular form, like the Church of the Holy Sepulchre at Jerusalem, in which the dead lay exposed to view on the days which preceded their interment; sometimes it was a hollow column ascended by a winding stair inside, or by projections left for the purpose within. It must have been a striking sight, when the traveller through the dark night saw far away the lonely flame that marked the spot where so many of his fellow-men had completed their journey.

The following extract from a paper in the Camden Society's possession, shows somewhat of the forms observed by our London forefathers on occasion of funerals:—
"January 2. Mr. Cornelius Bee, bookseller, in Little Britain, died *hora* xia, *ante merid*, his 2 eldest daughters, Mis Horwood and Mis Fletcher, widdows, executrixes, buried Jan. 4, at Great St. Bartholemew's without a sermon, without wine or wafers, only cloves and rosemary. Dr. Wells of Aldersgate read ye service. His younger daughter married to Nath Hook, his servant."—"June 30. This Sunday in the afternoone died John Smith, alderman of London and justice of peace in Middlesex, at his house in Finsbury, his funerall the 16th July from Goldsmith's Hall to Criplegate church, where he was interred with a sermon by Dr. Prichard, our vicar. The posie of his rings 'Ever Last.' He made a great gaine by musk catts which he kept."—"July 21. Samuel Crumbleholme, schoolmaster of Paul's school, died, buried ye 26. Dr. Wells of Aldersgate, preached his funerall sermon at my Lord Mayor's chapell by Guildhall. Rings were given, whose posie was '*Redime Tempus.*'"

Many relations might be given of funerals having been solemnized within the church porch. Audry, who died of the pestilence in the year 669, and Chad, who did not outlive the year 672, with other persons of that era, of extraordinary reputed sancity, being anxious to creep near the church, were the first placed there. Among the many legends relative to St. Swithin, there is one stating that his corpse, not being allowed to enter the church, was placed in the church porch, where it remained forty days, during which time it rained incessantly. This account agrees in some measure with the Latin legend quoted in Lord Campbell's " Lives of the Chancellors," which William of Malmesbury has given us as a proof of St. Swithin's great humility :—" For when he was about to bid farewell to this life, he gave orders to be buried outside the church, exposed to the rain dropping from the skies, and the treading of the passers by," and so he continued for some time ; but the ecclesiastics not liking that a person of his sancity should be so exposed, dug him up, when it is possible that, agreeably with his desire to be buried outside the church, they placed him in the porch.

The Churchwarden's account of Banwell, Somersetshire, contains the following curious items :—" 1521. Recd. of Robert Cabzll, for lyying of his wyffe in the *porch*, 3s. 4d. Recd. of Robert Blundon, for lyying of his wyffe in the *church*, 6s. 8d." By which it appears that the fee was as much again for burying in the church as in the porch.

There is a curious custom in Lower Brittany, which we may perhaps seek in vain elsewhere. As there is a *Basvalau* for the weddings, a rhymer for the merry festivals, there is at the same time a *paterer* to pray before the coffin, who is both a poet and improvisatore. He knows how to adapt ancient prayers in verse to the character and position of the departed. In this gloomy poetry there are sometimes bold, strange, and striking images. They frequently give the words as from the corpse itself, which from the interior of its bier is supposed to address to the living lamentations of grief, and austere recommendations. "It is Jesus," says one of these exhortations, "who has sent me to rouse you from your lethargy, unite your prayers to the prayers of souls. Pray, relations; pray, friends; for the children do not. Dear friends, pray; for children are very ungrateful. A white sheet, four planks, a straw pillow under the head, and five feet of earth, therein behold the wealth of this world. Perhaps your father, your mother, perhaps your brother, your sister, are scorching in purgatory. There, on bended knees, flames above, flames below, they cry out to you— Prayers, prayers." The effect of these compositions, recited in a slow, solemn, and mournful tone, amid tears, sobs, and groans, is extraordinary. .

In the southern parts of Northamptonshire may still be witnessed the poetical custom of placing garlands of flowers within a coffin, before it is deposited in the grave. When the corpse is that of an elderly person, the blossoms are mingled with sprigs of box and yew.

A grave, wherever found, preaches a short and pithy lesson to the soul, and it is well for us occasionally to pass an hour in the silence of God's acre, as a species of soul exercise or mental physic, to remind us of the great aims and objects of a true man's life, and we cannot do better than quote the exquisite reflections of Addison on this subject :—"When I look upon the tombs of the great, every emotion of envy dies within me; when I read the epitaphs of the beautiful, every inordinate desire goes out; when I meet with the grief of parents upon a tombstone, my heart melts with compassion; when I see the tombs of the parents themselves, I consider the vanity of grieving for those whom we must quickly follow; when I see kings lying side by side, or the holy men that divided the world with their contests and disputes, I reflect with sorrow and astonishment on the little competitions, factions, and debates of mankind; when I read the several dates of the tombs, of some that died yesterday, and some six hundred years ago, I consider that great day when we shall all of us be contemporaries, and make our appearance together."

But to some, alas, tablets nor tombstones gratify the sight, nor call to mind any sweet recollections of the past. How sad a reflection is a burial at sea! there are few more impressive ceremonies, and yet we would not that any friend of ours should sleep his last sleep among the unknown caverns of the mighty ocean. It is a satisfaction, although a melancholy one, to know the exact spot where the mortal remains of those we have loved in life are deposited,—to repair to the old churchyard when the dreary winter months have passed away, and plant the earliest flowers of spring upon their graves, to meditate and weep there, to think of the past, and hope for the future, the earnest heartfelt hope of all who well and truly believe, that they may be re-united at that day, when the sea and the dry land shall alike give up their dead. All this is comfort; but once sunk beneath the surface of the ocean, how shall we mark the spot where the body lies?

We quote the following lines on a burial at sea, from an anonymous author :—

The solemn words are said, "Let the sea receive the dead
   In its vast unfathomed bed, until Time shall be no more."
The frothing of a wave, and the good, the kind, the brave,
   Is in his ocean grave—all his storms of life are o'er.

His messmates stare with eyes of dull and long surprise,
   That where their comrade lies, not a trace should now be seen.
The waves still roll and leap o'er the chamber of his sleep,
   Down, down in the great deep, as though he had never been.

His messmates walk away, and in hoarse whispers say,
   "God rest him;" so they pray. Who doubts this prayer is heard?
When seated at their mess, they found one face the less,
   Each shows his kind distress, though he does not speak a word.

Some think that when again they cross that restless main,
   They'll look and look in vain for their messmate's place of rest,
And some will sadly sigh, and wish that when they die,
   In churchyard they may lie, with those they have loved the best.

Death will not come and go without his fitting woe;
   Methinks 'tis doubly so when he meets us on the sea.
The world is then so small, a ship contains its all;
   The dead man 'neath the pall, how large a part was he!

The sorrow for the dead is the only sorrow from which we refuse to be divorced; in pure grief we are all equal. Where is the mother who would willingly forget her child, though every recollection is a pang? Where is the child that would willingly forget the most tender of parents? who, even in the hour of agony, would forget the friend over whom he mourns? who, even when the tomb is closing upon the remains of her he most loved, when he feels his heart pierced with agony, would accept of consolation that must be bought by forgiveness? No; the love which survives the tomb is one of the noblest attributes of the soul. If it has its woes, it has likewise its delights; and when the overwhelming burst of grief is calmed into the gentle tear of recollection—when the sudden anguish and the convulsive agony over the present ruins of all that we most loved, is softened away into pensive meditation on all that it was in the days of its loveliness, who would root out such a sorrow from the heart, though it may sometimes throw a passing cloud over the bright hour of gaiety, or spread a deeper sadness over the hour of gloom? Yet who would exchange it, even for the song of pleasure or the burst of revelry? At the grave of those we love, we call up in long review the whole history of virtue and gentleness, and the thousand endearments lavished upon us, almost unheeded in the past daily course of intimacy; there it is that we dwell upon the tenderness, the solemn awful tenderness of the parting scene, and the last feeble fluttering, thrilling—oh, how thrilling—pressure of the hand, the last fond look of the glazing eye turning upon us even from the threshold of existence, the faint faltering accents struggling in death to give one more assurance of affection.

It is in the churchyard, with its leafy elms, its daisied graves, where angels seem to throng around us, and to whisper mighty secrets of the mysteries of the future world. It is there, beside the grave of buried love, we should meditate and settle with our conscience for every past benefit unrequited, every past endearment unregarded, of that departed being who can never—never—never return to be soothed by our contrition. If thou art a child, and hast ever added a sorrow to the soul, or a furrow to the silvered brow of an affectionate parent—if thou art a husband, and hast ever wronged the fond bosom that ventured its whole happiness in thy truth—

if thou art a friend, and hast ever wronged, in thought, or word, or deed, the spirit that generously confided in thee— if thou art a lover, and hast ever given one unmerited pang to that true heart which now lies cold and still beneath thy feet—then, be sure that every unkind look, every ungracious word, every ungentle action will come thronging back upon memory, and knocking dolefully at thy soul,—then, be sure that thou wilt lie down sorrowing and repentant on the grave, and utter the unheard groan, and pour the unavailing tear;—*then,* weave thy chaplet of flowers, and strew the beauties of nature about the grave, console thy broken spirit, if thou canst, but take warning by the bitterness of thy contrite affliction over the dead, and henceforth be more faithful and affectionate in the discharge of thy duties to the living.

We see the presence of God in all that we meet with; no matter where it may be, we see His work in some particular form. Passing through a churchyard—ground hallowed by the departed—we call to mind the many who are left to deplore the loss of some kindred spirit. What we see in that sacred spot should make us feel all our worldliness, and what we must be. Tombstones are but records of earthly feeling and regrets; it is at His tribunal, and to His mercy, that our names are made glorious and everlasting. From the creation to the present time, man has degenerated in that one imperative duty—act strictly in the discharge of your natural dictates, forgive your enemies, do not glory at their downfall, but remember that in a very short period you and all your acquaintances will be on equal terms. If you feel a bitter thought towards your fellow-man, walk through a burial place, and therein you will read a moral lesson.

We move among the green hillocks, wondering who lie beneath them, and whether they are entirely forgotten by the busy world that they left behind them; and as we muse on the transitory nature of this present life, the prayer instinctively rises to our lips, "So teach us to number our days, that we may apply our hearts unto wisdom." "Let me die the death of the righteous, and let my last end be like his."

It cannot, however, be said that the inscriptions chiselled on the various tombstones are always aids to reflection. In some cases they offend our taste; in others they excite our merriment. What a pity it is in so solemn a place, and in connection with so grave a subject, we should meet with so many absurd and unseemly observations! Even where the rhymes are decent, the theology is often sadly defective; and we are sorry for the friends of the departed, if they had no better ideas associated with the memories of their lost ones, than those which are embodied in their epitaphs.

I.

Elegant Epitaphs.

In *Brading* Church, *Isle of Wight*, is the celebrated epitaph by Mrs. STEELE:—

> Forgive, blest shade! the tributary tear,
>   That mourns thy exit from a world like this;
> Forgive the wish that would have kept thee here,
>   And stayed thy progress to the seats of bliss!
>
> No more confined to grovelling scenes of night,
>   No more a tenant pent in mortal clay,
> Now should we rather hail thy glorious flight,
>   And trace thy journey to the realms of day!

The following epitaph is in *West Moulsey* Churchyard, on SPENCER PERCEVAL CROKER, who died when a boy three years old:—

> Oh, pity us! who lost, when Spencer died,
> Our child, our hope, our pleasure, and our pride!
> In him we saw, or fancied, all such youth
> Could show of talents, tenderness, and truth.

And hoped to other eyes his ripened powers,
Would keep the promise they had made to ours;
But God a different, better growth has given—
The seed He planted here now blooms in heaven.

Epitaph on CARRIE, aged fifteen :—

O cruel Death! thy breath hath chilled
   The fairest flower God e'er gave,
   And laid in yonder silent grave
The broken voice for ever stilled!
Carrie, the sweetest, fairest one—
   A rose beneath a summer sky —
   It was so hard that she should die,
And hard to say, "Thy will be done!"
Ah, no, the smiles come through my tears;
   The cold gray stone, the speechless mound
   Hath yet a voice—"I now have found
The Life of Love which hath no years!"

In *Sheffield* general cemetery is this epitaph on a young lady :—

Ye who have mourned a sister's early doom,
Or bent in sorrow o'er a daughter's tomb,
Oh, weep for those who sadly now deplore
The fate, the virtues, of a maid no more!
What power can soothe a tender parent's grief,
Or bring the friends', the sisters', woes relief?
Religion pure, ineffably divine,
Angel of peace, that heavenly power is thine.

To the memory of LUCY LYTTLETON :—

Made to engage all hearts, and charm all eyes;
Tho' weak, magnanimous; tho' witty, wise;
Polite as all her life in courts had been,
Yet good as she the world had never seen;
The noble fire of an exalted mind
With gentle female tenderness combined;

Her speech was the melodious voice of love;
Her song the warblings of the vernal grove;
Her eloquence was sweeter than her song,
Soft as her heart, and as her reason strong;
Her form each beauty of her mind expressed;
Her mind was virtue by the Graces dressed.

On a whole family cut off by the small-pox :—

At once deprived of life, lies here
A family to virtue dear.
Though far removed from regal state,
Their virtues made them truly great.
Lest one should feel the other's fall,
Death has, in kindness, seized them all.

A beautiful inscription, it is said, may be found in an *Italian* churchyard :—

Here lies ESTELLA, who transported a large fortune to heaven in acts of charity, and has gone thither to enjoy it.

Kensington churchyard :—

Sacred to the memory of JAMES ELPHINSTONE.

His mind was ingenious, his heart was affectionate, his manners, though polished, were simple, his integrity was undeviating; he was a great scholar, and a real Christian. Jortin, Franklin, and Johnson were in the number of his friends. He was born at Edinboro', *Nov.* 25, O.S. 1721. He died at Hammersmith, *Oct.* 8, 1809, and his remains are deposited near the south side of this churchyard. In grateful remembrance of his virtues and affections, his widow has caused this tablet to be engraved.

Same place :—

ROBERT LORD VISCOUNT MOLESWORTH,
Departed this life *Jan.* 27, 1813, in his 84th year.

Awake, thou that sleepest. It is Jesus Christ that shall raise
you to Himself at the last day.

MARY ANN, VISCOUNTESS OF MOLESWORTH,
Died 2nd *August*, 1819, in the 82nd year of her age.

Welcome, sweet day of rest,.
Welcome to my Saviour's breast.

Same place :—

Sacred to the memory of
CAROLINE WILLIS, daughter of H. N. Willis, Esq.,
who died *March* 12, 1805, aged 17.

Sleep soft in dust until the Almighty will,
Then rise, unchanged, and be an angel still.

Same place :—

MR. THOMAS WRIGHT,
Died *March* 12, 1776, aged 67 years.

Farewell, vain world! I've had enough of thee,
I value not what thou canst say of me;
Thy smiles I value not, nor frowns don't fear,
All's one to me, my head is quiet here;
What faults you've seen in me, take care to shun,
Go home, and see there's something to be done.

Same place. On JOSEPH STEPHENSON, 26 *April*, 1765 :—

Where this rude stone in plaintive numbers weeps,
A friend, a father, and a husband sleeps;

A heart once glowing with the sacred flame
Of every duty, these relations claim ;
Of warm benevolence, and faith sincere.
Reader ! if worth, if virtue's self, be dear,
Mourn then their loss, for STEPHENSON lies here.

Same place :—

Sacred to the memory of
JAMES GUNTER, Esq., of Earls Court, Kensington,
who departed this life in the 74th year of his age.

When the ear heard him, then it blessed him ; and when the eye saw him, then it gave witness to him.

"The blessings of those who were ready to perish came upon him, and he caused the widow's heart to leap for joy."

October, 1819.

Same place :—

Here are deposited the remains of Mrs. ANN FLOYER, the beloved wife of Mr. Richard Floyer, of Thistle Grove, in this parish. Died on Thursday the 8th of *May*, 1823.

God hath chosen her as a pattern for the other angels.

In *Runcorn* Churchyard, near *Liverpool*, are two inscriptions, as follows :—

Mrs. JANET MORRISON, daughter of William Morrison, Esq., of Greenock, in North Britain, died at Runcorn, upon the sixth day of *February*, 1801, in the thirty-first year of her age.

This Stone
is erected by
Æneas Morrison,
the husband of
Mrs. JANET MORRISON,
to designate the spot
where her remains are
deposited, that her
infant children, when
they shall have attained
a more mature age,
may approach it with
reverential awe, and
pledge their vows to heaven
to respect her memory
by imitating her
virtues.

The second:—

Underneath this stone lie the remains of

ROBERT CHESHYRE, of *Rock-Savage*.

He departed this life *September* 9, 1802,

Aged 27 years.

'Tis *mine* to-day to moulder in the tomb,
To-morrow may *thy* awful summons come.
Wake, thou that sleepest, then; awake, or know
Thy dream will terminate in endless woe.
Wake, and contend for Heaven's immortal prize,
And give to God each moment as it flies.
Secure then mayst thou recollect the past,
And with a sacred triumph meet thy last.

At *Dover:*—

> Weep not, weep not, tho' I am gone,
>   For Christ thy afflicted heart will cheer;
> Weep not, weep not: thou art not alone;
>   Angels guard thy path, although so drear.

In the Churchyard of *Ashton*, near *Plymouth*, is an inscription to the memory of a dear wife:—

> In thy long sleep I'll watch thee as of yore,
> Until life fails, and then we'll part no more;
> O death, thy worst is done, and thy next blow
> Will join the hearts which thou hast severed now.

In the Chapel belonging to the *Foundling Hospital:*—

To the memory of
CAPTAIN THOMAS CORAM,
Whose name will never want a monument
so long as this Hospital shall subsist,
was born in the year 1668.
A man eminent in the most eminent virtue,
the love of mankind;
little attentive to his private fortune,
and refusing many opportunities of increasing it,
his time and thoughts were continually employed in
endeavours to promote the public happiness,
both in this kingdom and elsewhere,
particularly in the Colonies of North America,
and his endeavours were many times crowned
with the desired success.
His unwearied solicitation, for above 17 years together
(which would have baffled the patience and industry
of any man less zealous in doing good),

and his application to persons of distinction, of both sexes,
obtained at length the Charter of the Incorporation
(bearing date the 17th of *October*, 1739),
for the maintenance and education
of exposed and deserted young children,
by which many thousands of lives
may be preserved to the public, and employed in a
frugal and honest course of industry.
He died the 29th *March*, 1752, in the 84th year of his age,
poor in worldly estate, rich in good works,
and was buried, at his own desire, in the Vault
underneath this Chapel (the first there deposited), at
the east end thereof;
many of the governors and other gentlemen
attending the funeral to do honour to his memory.

READER,
Thy actions will show whether thou art sincere
in the praises thou mayest bestow on him;
And if thou hast virtue enough to commend his virtues,
forget not to add also the imitations of them.

In *Trevethin* Churchyard, *Monmouth*, is the following epitaph, written by Sir Charles Hanbury Williams, on a faithful servant of his father's :—

To the memory of
Mr. THOMAS COOKE,
Agent of the iron-works of *Pontypool*,
who died *August* 1st, 1739,
Aged 66 years.

With most religious truth it may be said,
Beneath this stone an honest man lies dead.

Vice he abhorred, in virtue's path he trod,
Just to his master, humble to his God.
Useful he lived, and void of all offence,
By nature sensible, well-bred by sense;
His master's interest was his constant end,
(The faithful'st servant, and the truest friend;)
For him his heart and hand were always join'd,
And love with duty strictly was combined.
Together through this vale of life they passed,
And in this church together sleep at last;
For when the master's fatal hour was come,
The servant sighed, and followed to the tomb;
And when at the last day he shall appear,
Thus shall his Saviour speak, and scatter fear,
"Well done, thou faithful servant, good and just,
Receive thy well-deserved reward of trust;
Come where no time can happiness destroy,
Into the fulness of thy Master's joy."

Gloucester Cathedral. On CATHERINE PEMBRUGE

Stop, traveller!
And learn from me
How vain the hopes, how transient the joys of men.
Here lies, alas! here lies my CATHERINE.
The best, the most excellent of wives,
So beautiful, so chaste, so loving,
That her superior did not exist.
If the loss of the youthful perfection,
Both in body and mind,
Be just subjects for sorrow,
Oh! tell me the end of my griefs.

WILLIAM PEMBRUGE, Gentleman,
Consecrated this Marble to the Memory of
His dear Wife, who died *June* 15, 1690, aged 24.

In *Woodhurst* Churchyard, near St. Ives, Huntingdonshire, on JOHN HILL, who died *January*, 1792, aged 20 years :—

> A youth is laid beneath this stone,
> Death nipped the bud, the blossom's gone.
> Be still, each parent's sighing heart,
> Time is but short that we shall part;
> When we again in glory meet,
> 'Twill turn past bitters all to sweet.

At the same place. On his Betrothed, SARAH ROYSTON, who died 1793, aged 23 years :—

> A pale consumption gave the fatal blow;
> The stroke was certain, though the effect was slow;
> With lingering pain Heaven saw me sore oppressed,
> Pitied my sighs, and kindly gave me rest.

In *Hoxton* Churchyard. To the memory of RICHARD PASSINGHAM, *August* 10th, 1852 :—

> Farewell, dear Husband, to my heart most dear,
> Oft shall I bathe thy memory with a tear;
> Farewell! it is thy death I so deplore,
> To mourn thy loss, but feel thou art no more.

From *Southam* Churchyard, *Warwickshire*. On JUDY TURVILL, aged 28 :—

> The Dame that takes her rest beneath this tomb,
> Had Rachel's face, and Leah's fruitful womb;
> Abigail's wisdom, Lydia's faithful heart,
> Martha's just care, and Mary's better part.

St. Pancras, Middlesex. On a lady :—

> Whate'er of mild affections was beloved,
> Revered of virtue, or of sense approved ;
> Whate'er of candour female bosoms know,
> Once warmed the gentle heart that rests below.
> Pure as that heart, may flowers eternal bloom,
> May pensive genius strew them round her tomb,
> And oh! may those by chance or fancy led
> To the sad mansions of the hallowed dead,
> With fond remembrance from this spot retire,
> And learn to copy what they must admire.

Same place :—

> Here innocence and beauty lie, whose breath
> Was snatched by early, not untimely death.
> Hence she did go, just as she did begin
> Sorrow to know, before she knew to sin.
> Death, that does sin and sorrow thus prevent,
> Is the next blessing to a life well spent.

Islip, Oxfordshire. On HANNAH and ELIZABETH, the Wives of Joseph Bridgewater :—

> Graves are lodgings to the blest,
> Not of horror, but of rest ;
> Cabinets that safely keep
> Mortal relics while they sleep.
> When the trump shall all awake,
> Every soul her flight shall take,
> And from that which putrefies
> Shall immortal bodies rise.
> In this faith they lived and died,
> In this hope they here reside.

Cheshunt, Hants. On WM. WILLIAMS, *Sept.* 24, 1782, aged 21 :—

> In silence here beneath a youth is laid,
> By whom the spots of nature were surveyed ;

With ravished breast, o'er meads he did pursue
The started hare, which through the landscape flew;
By which pursuit, his heart oppressed with heat,
Plunged in the stream which Nature thought so sweet;
But soon the stream a change to Nature gave,
And plunged this youth deep in the silent grave.

Epitaph by William Somerville (1730), upon HUGH LUMBER, a Warwickshire husbandman :—

In cottages and lonely cells
True piety neglected dwells,
Till called to heaven, her native seat,
Where the good man alone is great ;
'Tis then this humble dust shall rise,
And view his Judge with joyful eyes,
While haughty tyrants shrink afraid,
And call the mountains to their aid.

At *Wisbeach*. On an infant :—

Beneath, a sleeping infant lies,
 To earth her body's lent ;
More glorious she'll hereafter rise,
 Tho' not more innocent.
When the Archangel's trump shall blow,
 And souls to bodies join,
Millions will wish their lives below
 Had been as short as thine.

Epitaph to the memory of a young lady, who died aged 18 years :—

Here innocence and virtue lie, whose breath
Was snatched by early, not untimely death.
Hence did she go, just as she did begin
Sorrow to know, before she knew to sin.
Death, that doth sin and sorrow thus prevent,
Is the next blessing to a life well spent.

Corley Churchyard, *Warwickshire* :—

> These hillocks green, and mouldering bones,
> These gloomy tombs and lettered stones,
> One admonition here supply—
> Reader! art thou prepared to die?

In *Wimbledon* Churchyard. On a young woman :—

> In life's sweet opening dawn she sought her God,
> And the gay path of youth with caution trod ;
> In bloom of beauty humbly turned aside
> The incense Flattery offered to her pride.
> Her front with blushing modesty she bound,
> And on her lips the law of truth was found ;
> Fond to oblige, too gentle to offend,
> Beloved by all, to all the good a friend :
> The bad she censured by her life alone ;
> Blind to their faults, severe upon her own.
> In others' joys and griefs a part she bore,
> And with the needy shared her little store ;
> At distance viewed the world with pious dread,
> And to God's temple for protection fled ;
> There sought that peace which Heaven alone can give,
> And learned to die ere others learn to live.
> Though closed those eyes, by which all hearts were charmed ;
> Though every feature of each grace disarmed,
> Yet think not that her piety was vain ;
> Her soul survives, her virtues still remain :
> O'er vanquished death the immortal saint prevails,
> And opening heaven the new-born angel hails.

In *Tenby* Church. On JANE GRIFFITH, wife of Thomas Griffith, mariner :—

> When faithful friends descend into the dust,
> Grief's but a debt, and sorrows are but just ;
> Such cause had he to weep who freely pays
> His last sad tribute of his love and praise,

> Who mourns the best of wives, and best of friends,
> Where with affection diligence was joined;
> Mourns, but not murmurs; sighs, but not despairs;
> Feels as a man, but as a Christian bears.

In *Burrington* Church, Somersetshire, may be seen a monument to the memory of ALBINA, daughter of the Rev. H. Wylde, and wife of — Jackson, Esq., who perished in the wreck of the *Elizabeth*, off *Dunkirk*, Dec. 27, 1810. The following epitaph was written by Hannah More :—

> Fair, young, and happy, loving and beloved,
> A daughter cherished, and a wife approved;
> Such was Albina! where could life display
> A fairer promise of a prosperous day?
> Ah! treacherous calm! the sky was soon o'ercast,
> Loud was the surge, and direful was the blast;
> Not fond affection's grasping arm could save
> The floating victim from her watery grave.
> Thou sad survivor! rescued from the deep,
> Improve the respite, cease at length to weep:
> Prepare to meet her on that blissful shore
> Where storms shall beat, and friends shall part, no more.
> Heaven calls, Hope leads, and Faith triumphant saves,
> Through the dear might of Him who walked the waves,

In *Norwich*, on Mr. BRYANT LEWIS, who was murdered upon the *Heath*, near *Thetford, Sept.* 13, 1698 :—

> Fifteen wide wounds this stone veils from thine eyes,
> But, reader, hark! their voice doth pierce the skies.
> Vengeance, cried Abel's blood against cursed Cain,
> But better things spake Christ when He was slain.
> Both, both, cries Lewis's 'gainst his barbarous foe,
> Blood, Lord, for blood, but save his soul from woe.

At *Battersea* Church, on WILLIAM CURTIS, the author of several botanical works; died 7th *July*, 1799, aged 53 :—

While living herbs shall spring profusely wild,
  Or garden cherish all that's sweet and gay,
So long thy works shall please, dear Nature's child,
  So long thy memory suffer no decay.

Epitaph by the late Lord Palmerston, to his parents, in *Romsey* Abbey Church:—

To those who knew the tenour of their days,
'Twere worse than useless to recount their praise;
To those by whom their virtues were unknown,
For cold applause the picture would be shown;
And proud affection asks not for their bier
The carnal tribute of a stranger's tear.
With aching bosoms, and with bleeding hearts,
We marked those sighs with which the spirit parts;
Yet bowed submissive to the chastening rod,
Nor dared to question the decrees of God.
More blest to live they die, in Him who trust;
He deals His mercies when He calls the just.

Epitaph in the *Broadway* Churchyard, *Westminster*, on three children, who all died very early, the eldest being little more than three years of age:—

Three children, not dead, but sleeping lie,
With Christ they live above the sky;
Wash'd in His blood, and for His dress,
Christ's glorious robe of righteousness,
In which they shine more bright by far
Than sun, or moon, or morning star.
In Paradise they wing their way,
Blooming in one eternal day.

In *Bremhill* Churchyard (written by the Rev. W. L. Bowles):—

"O mother, I will rise and pray,"
  With feeble voice, she cried;
"For this, dear mother, is the day
  On which poor father died."

ELEGANT EPITAPHS. 37

> Faintly she spoke—she knelt, she pray'd,
>   Her eyes with weeping dim,
> And ere seven days had pass'd was laid
>   In the same grave with him.
>
> Oh! when all worlds before their God,
>   In trembling hope shall stand,
> She shall awake from the same sod,
>   And smile at His right hand.

On Mrs. M. PASTON, of *Barmingham*, in *Norfolk*, who died a short time after her marriage, in the 21st year of her age; written by John Dryden:—

> So fair, so young, so innocent, so sweet,
> Require at least an age in one to meet;
> In her they met, but long they could not stay,
> 'Twas gold too fine to fix without allay.
> Heaven's image was in her so well exprest,
> Her very sight upbraided all the rest;
> Too justly ravish'd from an age like this,
> Now *she* is gone, the world is of a piece.

Another:—

> Pilgrim! if youth's seductive bloom,
>   Thy soul in pleasure's vest arrays,
> Pause at this sad and silent tomb,
>   And learn how swift thy bliss decays.
> But ah! if woe has stabb'd thy breast,
>   And dimm'd with tears thy youthful eye,
> Mourner, the grave's a house of rest,
>   And this one teaches how to die;
> For she who sleeps this stone beneath,
>   Tho' many an hour to pain was given,
> Smiled at the hovering dart of death,
>   While hope display'd the joys of heaven.

Another:

> Bold Infidelity, turn pale and die;
> Under this stone an infant's ashes lie,
> Say, is it lost or saved?
> If death's by sin, it sinned, because 'tis here;
> If heaven's by works, it can't in heaven appear:
> Ah! Reason, how depraved!
> Revere the Bible's sacred page: the knot's untied;
> It died thro' Adam's sin; it lives—for Jesus died.

An *inscription* by Gilbert West, Esq. (1743), on the tomb raised to the memory of his father and ancestors in *Bedford*:—

> Unmark'd by trophies of the great and vain,
> Here sleep within this tomb a gentle train;
> No folly wasted their paternal store,
> No guilt nor sordid avarice made it more.
> With honest fame and sober plenty crowned,
> They lived, and spread their cheering influence round.
> May he whose hand this pious tribute pays,
> Receive a like return of filial praise!

In the Churchyard of *St. Andrew's the Less, Cambridge*, on — STEWART, who died 1772, aged 46 years, and can be seen on a tombstone at *Ecclesfield*, near *Sheffield*:—

> Man's life is like a winter's day:
> Some only breakfast, and away;
> Others to dinner stay, and are well fed;
> The oldest man but sups, and goes to bed.
> Long is his life who lingers out the day,
> Who goes the soonest has the least to pay.

We have seen this epitaph also in *Llangollen* Churchyard, with the two last lines thus:—

> Such is our lot—We linger out the day;
> Who stays the longest has the most to pay.

In the Chapel belonging to *Guy's Hospital* is the following inscription:—

Underneath are deposited the remains of THOMAS GUY, Citizen of London, Member of Parliament, and the sole founder of this Hospital in his lifetime. It is peculiar to this beneficent man to have persevered, during a long course of prosperity and industry, in pouring forth to the wants of others all that he had earned by labour or withheld from self-indulgence. Warm with philanthropy, and exalted by charity, his mind expanded to those noble affections which grow but too rarely from the most elevated pursuits. After administering with extensive bounty to the claims of consanguinity, he established this Asylum for that stage of languor and disease to which the charity of others had not reached. He provided a retreat for hopeless insanity, and rivalled the endowment of kings. He died the 27th of *December*, 1724, in the 80th year of his age.

At *St. Mary Overey, Borough*, in the arch between the north aisle and the altar, under a canopy with roses, supported by Ionic pillars, are figures of a man, two females, and children, all kneeling. The inscription informs us that the monument is to the pious memory of RICHARD HUMBLE, Alderman of London, and several members of his family, which information is succeeded by the following lines :—

> Like the damask Rose you see,
> Or like the Blossom on the tree,
> Or like the dainty Flower of May,
> Or like the morning of the Day,

Or like the Sun, or like the Shade,
Or like the Gourd which Jonas had,
Even so is MAN, whose thread is spun,
Drawn out and cut, and so is done.
Ye Rose withers, ye Blossom blasteth,
Ye Flower fades, ye MORNING hasteth,
Ye Sun sets, ye Shadow flies,
Ye Gourd consumes, and Man he dies.

Tring, Hertfordshire. On Dame ELIZABETH GORE :—

Here lieth the Body of
Dame ELIZABETH,
Late Wife of SIR WILLIAM GORE, Knt.,
Descended from worthy ancestors,
Whose honoured Names are not recited,
Because she wanted no borrowed Lustre,
Being adorned with all Graces and Perfections,
Both of Body and Mind.
She was Pious and Devout,
Wise and Virtuous,
A faithful and obedient Wife,
A prudent and tender Mother.
To her Friends,
Kind and useful, courteous and sincere ;
To the Poor,
Compassionate, and full of good Works.
A singular Modesty, Meekness, and Humility
Appeared in all her Words and Actions,
And her Life
Was a fair Example of amiable and illustrious Virtues
In every Relation.
After a short sickness, on the 4th of *March*,

She humbly resigned her pious Soul to God,
1705, Æt. 52.
This Monument is erected for a lasting Memorial
Of his Parents,
By William Gore, Esq.

At *Coleshill, Warwickshire.* On LADY MARY DIGBY
(by Dr. Hough, Bishop of Worcester) :—

MARY, Relict of KILDARE LORD DIGBY,
Departed this life, *Dec.* 23,
Anno Dom. 1692.
Whom it were unpardonable to lay down in Silence,
And of whom 'tis difficult to speak with Justice,
For her Just Character will look like Flattery,
And the least abatement of this is injury to her Memory.
In every Condition of Life she was a Pattern to her Sex ;
Appeared Mistress of those peculiar Qualities
That were requisite to conduct her thro' it with Honour,
And never failed to exert them in their proper Seasons
With the utmost Advantage.
She was Modest without Affectation,
Easy without Levity, and Reserved without Pride,
Knew how to stoop without sinking,
And to gain People's Affections without lessening their
Regards.
She was Careful without Anxiety,
Frugal without Parsimony ;
Not at all fond of the superfluous Trappings of Greatness,
Yet abridged herself in nothing that her Quality required.
She was a faithful member of the Church of England ;
Her piety was exemplary, her Charity universal ;

She found herself a Widow, in the beginning of her Life,
When the Temptations of Beauty, Honour, Youth,
and Pleasure,
Were in their full strength ;
Yet she made them all give way to the Interest of her
Family,
And betook herself entirely to the Matron's Part.
The Education of her Children engrossed all her Cares,
No charge was spared in the Cultivation of their Minds,
Nor pains in the Improvement of their Fortunes.
In a word,
She was truly Wise, truly Honourable, and truly Good.
More can scarce be said,
And yet he that says this knew her well,
And is well assured he has said nothing
Which either Veracity or Modesty should oblige him to
suppress.

The following epitaph was copied from a tombstone in the Churchyard of *Longside*, near *Peterhead*, and is believed to be from the pen of the Rev. John Skinner, better known as the author of "Tullochgorum" :—

> And she is gone ! the once so lovely maid
> Gone hence, and now a dear departed shade,
> Call'd from this world in early dawn of life,
> When but beginning to be called a wife.
> Ye virgin tribe, whom chance may lead this way,
> Where brightest beauty moulders into clay,
> Behold this stone, nor be ashamed to mourn
> Awhile o'er Mary Alexander's urn.
> She who lies here was once like one of you,
> Youthful and gay, and fair as you are now.
> One week beheld her a fair blooming bride,
> In marriage pomp laid by a husband's side ;

The next week saw her in death's livery drest,
And brought her breathless body here to rest.
Not all this world's gay hopes, nor present charms,
Nor parent's tear, nor a fond husband's arms,
Could stamp the least impression on her mind,
Or sink to earth a soul for heaven design'd.
Calmly she left a scene so lately tried ;
Heaven call'd her home, with pleasure she complied
Embraced her sorrowing friends, then smiled, and died.

St. Margaret's, Westminster (by Pope) :—

In Memory of
MRS. ELIZABETH CORBETT,
Who departed this life at *Paris, March* 1st, 1724,
After a long and painful sickness.
She was Daughter of SIR UVEDALE CORBETT,
Of *Longnor*, in the County of *Salop*, Bart.,
By the Right Honourable the LADY MILDRED CECILL,
Who ordered this Monument to be erected.

Here rests a Woman, good without Pretence,
Blest with plain Reason, and with sober Sense :
No Conquest she, but o'er herself desired ;
No arts essay'd, but not to be admired.
Passion and Pride were to her Soul unknown,
Convinced that Virtue only is our own.
So unaffected, so composed a mind,
So firm, yet soft, so strong, yet so refined,
Heaven as its purest Gold, by Tortures try'd,
The Saint sustain'd it, but the *Woman* dy'd.

East Hampstead, Berkshire. On Mr. ELIJAH FENTON, the poet, 1731 (Pope) :—

This modest stone, what few vain marbles can,
May truly say, Here lies an honest man!
A Poet bless'd beyond the Poet's Fate,
Whom Heaven kept sacred from the proud and great,
Foe to loud Praise, and Friend to learned Ease,
Content with Science in the Vale of Peace,
Calmly he look'd on either Life, and here,
Saw nothing to regret, or there to fear,
From Nature's temp'rate Feast rose satisfy'd,
Thank'd Heav'n that he had lived and that he dy'd.

Epitaph :—

"Weep not," ye mourners, for the dead,
  But in this hope your spirits soar,
That ye can say of those ye mourn,
  They are not lost, but gone before.

Christ to the widow'd mother said,
  "Weep not," and thus He healed her pain;
And now to ye who mourn, He says,
  "Weep not," ye all shall meet again.

And in this hope we live, that death,
  Who plucks from earth its fairest flowers,
Doth give them back to God again,
  To plant in brighter lands than ours.

Epitaph on the grave of the "Dairyman's Daughter" (*vide* Leigh Richmond's "Annals of the Poor"), and may be seen in the Churchyard of *St. Sidwell's, Exeter*, near the south-east end of the Church, and *Mount Jerome* Cemetery, *Dublin* :—

  This lovely bud, so young and fair,
    Call'd hence by early doom,
  Just came to show how sweet a flower
    In Paradise might bloom.

In *Arreton* Church, *Isle of Wight*, the subjoined may be seen on the tomb of W. SERLE :—

>Loe, here vnder this tombe incovtch'd,
> Is William Serle by name,
>Who for his deedes of charetie
> Deserveth worthey fame.
>
>A man within this parish borne,
> And in the howse call'd Stone,
>A glasse for to behowld a work
> Hath left to everey one.
>
>For that vnto the people poore
> Of Arreton he gave
>An hvndred powndes in redie coyne,
> He willd that they showld have.
>
>To be employ'd in fittest sort,
> As man could best invent,
>For yearelie relief to the poore,
> That was his good intent.
>
>Thus did this man, a batcheler,
> Of yeares full fiftey-nyne,
>And doeinge goode to maney a one,
> Soe did he spend his tyme,
>
>Vntill the day he did decease,
> The first of Febrvarey,
>And in the yeare of One thousand
> Five hvndred neyntie-fyve.

At *Boughton*, near *Northampton*, the following epitaph may be seen :—

>Time was I stood where thou dost now,
> And view'd the dead, as thou dost me;
>Ere long thou'lt be as low as I,
> And others stand and look on thee.

In the north aisle of *St. Giles'* Church, *Cripplegate:*—

A remembrance of THOMAS BVSBY,
Cooper and Citizen of London, who departed this life in
Ano 1575, and bvried heare the xi. of July.

This BVSBY, willing to relieve the poore with fire and with breade,
Did give that hovse in which he dy'd, then called the Queenes heade.
Foure full loades of ye best charcole he wovld have bovght each yeare,
And fortie dosen of wheaten breade, for poor hovseholders heare.
To see these things distribvted, this BVSBY put in trvst
The Vicar and Chvrchwardens, thinking them to be jvst.
God grante that poor hovseholders heare may thankfvl be for svch,
So God will move ye heartes of more, to do for them as mvch;
And let this good example move such men as God has blest,
To do the like before they goe with BVSBY to their reste.
Within this chappell BVSBY'S bones in dvst awhile doth stay,
Till He that made them, raise them up to live with Christ for aye.

In *St. Mary's* Churchyard, *Rotherhithe,* is a monument to the memory of PRINCE LEE BOO, buried here 27th *December*, 1784, aged 20. He was an amiable young man, son of Abba Thule Rupack, King of Coo-roo-ras, one of the Pelew group of Islands in the Indian Ocean. The Honourable East India Company had the following inscribed as a testimony of the humane and kind treatment afforded by his father to the crew of their ship *Antelope* wrecked on that shore. Captain Wilson, the commander, brought over Lee Boo to be educated, but he unfortunately died at the above early age:—

Stop, reader, stop,
Let Nature claim a tear.
A Prince of "mine,"
LEE BOO, lies buried here.

In the Church of *Esher, Surrey,* is a brass plate fixed to a stone, with the effigies of a man and woman, and it is recorded that—

> The XXIX. in anno six and seventye
> Above V. hundred three times told,
> Did WILLIAM WICKER dye.
>
> He dying gave to God his soule,
> His body here to rest.
> The corpes in yearthe, the soule I trust
> Is placed among the blest.

The following epitaph marks the grave of a youthful but devoted Christian :—

> In Memory of
> ANNE C. MAURICE,
> Who entered into glory *February* 16th, 1826,
> trusting solely in the finished work of her God and Saviour,
> Jesus Christ.
> Reader! on what is your trust placed?

On the death of GEORGE CHERRIMAN, who died suddenly in a field, *August,* 1817, aged 69 :—

> Stop, passenger, and, wrapt in thought,
> The realms of death survey.
> Till by the view reflective taught,
> You learn to live to-day.
>
> How vain is life! to-morrow's dawn
> Perhaps you ne'er may see;
> Between—how slight the curtain's drawn—
> Eternity and thee!

On a plain marble stone is this brief inscription :—

> She always made home happy.

At Wirhsworth, Derbyshire :—

RICHARD FAIRWEATHER EATON, son of James and Eizabeth Eaton, died *November* 30th, 1850, aged 7 years and 10 months.

> Step soft, ye youth, on hallow'd ground ye tread,
> And not disturb the mansions of the dead.
> A youth lies here seclused in peaceful dust,
> Whose steps were virtue, and his actions just.
> By all esteem'd, yea, and by all approved,
> He died lamented, as he lived beloved."

Epitaph found among the ruins of *Melrose* Abbey, *Roxburghshire ;*—

> Earth walketh on the earth,
>   Glistening like gold,
> Earth goeth to the earth
>   Sooner than it wold.
> Earth buildeth on the earth
>   Palaces and towers ;
> Earth saith to the earth,
>   "All shall be ours."

In the chancel of *Mullion* Church, *Cornwall*, is a tablet to the memory of THOMAS FLAVEL, a former vicar, and on a piece of brass are the following lines :—

> Earth, take thine earth ; my sin let Satan havet ;
> The world my goods ; my soul my God who gavet :
> For from these four—Earth, Satan, World, and God—
> My Flesh, my Sin, my Goods, my Soul I had.

In *Belper* Churchyard :—

> Oh, cruel death! who could no longer spare
> A loving father and a tender mother dear;
> The loss is great to them that's left behind,
> They're gone in hopes eternal joys to find.

Another memorial to a departed parent :—

> Our Mother
> Fell Asleep
> *Nov.* 12th, 1840,
> Æ. 41.
> When will morning come?

In *Derby* Old Cemetery :—

> A better husband never lived,
> A kinder father never died,
> This honest heart no man deceived,
> His manly spirit knew no pride.
> His memory fondly in our hearts shall rest,
> Loved while on earth, in heaven for ever blest.

St. Peter's, St. Alban's. On RICHARD SKYPWITH :—

In the yere of Christ, on Thousand Fowr Hundry'd ful trew, wyth
    Fowr and Sixteen,
I Richard Skypwith, Gentleman in Birth, late fellow of
    New Inne,
In my age Twenti-on, my Sowl party'd from the Body in August
    the 16th day,
And now I ly here, abyding God's mercy, under this ston
    in clay,
Desiring you that this sal see, unto the *Meyden* pray for me,
    That bare both God and Man,
Like as ye wold, that oder for ye shold
    When ye ne may nor can.

From an ancient manuscript in the British Museum :—

In the Cathedrall Churche of *St. Paule*, in *London*, a stone is inscribed thus, without a name :—

>Non nominem aspiciam
>ultra
>Oblivio.

This man woulde nott willingly have forgotten, when he adjoyned his armes to continue his memorye.

Another, lykewyse suppressing his name, for his epitaph, did sett downe this goodly admonition :—

>Looke, man, before thee, how thy death hastethe;
>Looke, man, behind thee, how thy lyfe wastethe;
>Looke on thy right side, how death thee desirethe;
>Looke on thy left side, how synne thee beguylethe;
>Looke, man, above thee—the joys that ever shall laste;
>Looke, man, beneathe thee, the paynes without reste.

In *Stoke* Church, near *Guildford :—*

This Monument was erected by Harriet Aldersey, in grateful remembrance of the most affectionate of husbands, WILLIAM ALDERSEY, Esq., of *Stoke* Park, a place formed by his taste, enlivened by his cheerfulness, made happy by his bounty, and better by his example. He departed this life 30th of *May*, 1800, aged 64 years.

>More would you have? go ask the poor he fed,
>Whose was the hand that raised their drooping head;
>Ask of the few whose path is strew'd with flowers,
>Who made the happy still have happier hours;
>Whose voice like his could charm all care away,
>Whose look so tender, or whose smile so gay:
>Go ask of all—and learn from ev'ry tear,
>The Good how honour'd, and the Kind how dear.

In *Père la Chaise*, near *Paris* :—

> MARIE was the only child of her mother,
> "And she was a widow."
> MARIE sleeps in this grave,
> And the widow has now no child.
>
> There was a sweet and nameless grace,
> That wander'd o'er the lovely face ;
> And from the pensive eyes of blue,
> Was magic in the glance which flew.
>
> Her hair in soft and glowing shade,
> In rich luxuriance curling stray'd ;
> But when she spoke, or when she sung,
> Enchantment on her accents hung.
>
> Where is she now ? Where all must be,
> Sunk in the grave's obscurity.
> Yet never, never slumber'd there,
> A mind more pure, a form more fair.

At *Kilravock, Ireland*. On MISS ROSE, Niece to Hugh Rose, Esq. :—

> Here lies a Rose, a budding Rose,
>   Blasted before its Bloom,
> Whose Innocence did sweets disclose,
>   Beyond that Flower's Perfume.
> To those who for her Loss are grieved,
>   This Consolation's given,
> She's from a world of woe relieved,
>   And blooms a Rose in Heaven.

Epitaph, by John Gay (1732) :—

> If e'er sharp sorrow from thine eyes did flow,
> If e'er thy bosom felt another's woe,
> If e'er fair beauty's charms thy heart did prove,
> If e'er the offspring of thy virtuous love,

Bloom'd to thy wish, or to thy soul was dear,
This plaintive marble asks thee for a tear.
For here, alas! too early snatch'd away,
All that was lovely Death has made his prey.
No more her cheeks with crimson roses vie,
No more the diamond sparkles in her eye,
Her breath no more its balmy sweets can boast;
Alas! that breath with all its sweets is lost.
Pale now those lips, where blushing rubies hung,
And mute the charming music of her tongue.
Ye virgins fair, your fading charms survey;
She was whate'er your tender hearts can say.
To her sweet memory, for ever dear,
Let the green turf receive your trickling tear.
To this sad place your earliest garlands bring,
And deck her grave with firstlings of the spring;
Let opening roses, drooping lilies tell,
Like those she bloom'd, and ah! like those she fell.
In circling wreathes let the pale ivy grow,
And distant yews a sable shade bestow.
Round her, ye Graces, constant vigil keep,
And guard, fair Innocence! her sacred sleep,
Till that bright morn shall make the beauteous clay
To bloom and sparkle in eternal day.

In *English College, Rome :—*

MARTHA SWINBURNE, born *Oct.* X. M.D.CCLXVIII, died *Sept.* VIII. M.D.CCLXXVIII. Her years were few, but her life was long and full. She spoke English, French, and Italian, and had made some progress in the Latin tongue; knew the English and Roman Histories, arithmetic, and geography; sang the most difficult music at sight, with one of the finest voices in the world; was a proficient on the harpsichord, wrote well, danced many sorts of dances with strength and elegance. Her face was beautiful and majestic, her body a perfect model, and all her motions graceful. Her docility, and alacrity in doing everything to make her parents happy, could only be equalled by her sense and aptitude. With so many perfections, amidst the praises of all persons, from the sovereign down to the beggar in the street, her heart was incapable of vanity. Affectation and arrogance were unknown to her. Her beauty and accomplishments rendered her the admiration of all beholders, the love of all that enjoyed her company. Think, then, what the pangs of her wretched parents must be at so cruel a separation. Their only comfort is in the certitude of her being completely happy, beyond the reach of pain, and for ever freed from the miseries of this life. She can never feel the torments they endure for the loss of a beloved child. Blame them not for indulging an innocent pride in transmitting her memory to posterity, as an honour to her family and her native country, England. Let this plain character, penned by her disconsolate father, claim a tear of pity from every eye that peruses it.

In the Churchyard of the *Gray Friars, Edinburgh,* commemorating the martyrs of the Covenant :—

> Halt, passenger! take heed what you do see.
> Here lies interred the dust of those who stood
> 'Gainst perjury, resisting unto blood,
> Adhering to the Covenant, and laws
> Establishing the same ; which was the cause
> Their lives were sacrificed unto the lust
> Of prelatists abjured, though here their dust

Lies mix'd with murderers and other crew
Whom justice justly did to death pursue ;
But as for them, no cause was to be found
Worthy of death, but only they were found
Constant and steadfast, witnessing
For the prerogatives of Christ their King ;
Which truths were seal'd by famous Guthrie's head,
And all along to Mr. Kenwick's blood,
They did endure the wrath of enemies,
Reproaches, torments, deaths, and injuries ;
But yet they're those who from such troubles came,
And triumph now in glory with the Lamb.

From *May* 27th, 1661, when the Marquis of Argyle was beheaded, to *February* 17th, 1688, when Mr. James Kenwick suffered, there were some eighteen thousand one way or other murdered, of whom were executed at *Edinburgh* about one hundred noblemen, ministers, and gentlemen, and others, noble martyrs for Christ. On a portion of rising ground, near the village of *Minnyshire*, was erected in 1828 a monument in commemoration of JAMES KENWICK, the last of the Scottish martyrs. He was only 27 when he was found guilty and executed at *Edinburgh*.

In the Parish Church of *North Berwick* a handsome altar tomb, supported by monumental pillars, is erected to the memory of the Rev. JOHN BLACKADDER, who died on the *Bass Rock*, near *Haddington* (John Knox, the celebrated Reformer, was a native of this place), in confinement, a martyr for conscience' sake.

In the parish of *Glencross, Scotland*, is a martyr's tomb, thus inscribed :—

ELEGANT EPITAPHS. 55

Here and near to this place lie the Rev. JOHN CRUICK-
SHANKS and Mr. ANDREW MAC CORMACH, ministers of
the Gospel, and about fifty other true covenanted Presby-
terians, who were killed in this place in their own innocent
self-defence, and in defence of the covenanted work of
reformation, by Thomas Dalziel, of Binns.

REV. xii. 11.
And they overcome by the blood of the Lamb, and by the word
of their testimony, and they loved not their lives unto the death.

Erected *September*, 1738.

On a Friend, by Robert Burns :—

> An honest man lies here at rest
> As ever God with His image blest;
> The friend of man, the friend of truth;
> The friend of age, the guide of youth:
> Few hearts like his, with virtue warm'd,
> Few heads with knowledge so inform'd.
> If there's another world, he lives in bliss;
> If there is none, he made the best of this.

In the Churchyard of *Lloughor*, in *Glamorganshire*, is
the following epitaph, containing an allusion to the interesting custom of strewing the grave with flowers :—

> The village maidens to her grave shall bring
> Selected garlands each returning spring ;
> Selected sweets, in emblem of the maid
> Who underneath this hallow'd turf is laid:
> Like her they flourish, beauteous to the eye ;
> Like her, too soon they languish, fade, and die.

On the daughter of Admiral PARKER, who died aged 15. She was cousin to Lord Byron, who composed her epitaph in 1802 :—

> Hushed are the winds, and still the evening gloom,
>   Not e'en a zephyr wanders through the grove,
> Whilst I return to view my Margaret's tomb,
>   And scatter flowers on the dust I love.
>
> Within this narrow cell reclines her clay:
>   That clay where once such animation beam'd;
> The King of Terrors seized her as his prey:
>   Nor worth nor beauty have her life redeem'd.
>
> Oh, could that King of Terrors pity feel,
>   Or Heaven reverse the dread decrees of Fate;
> Not here the mourner would his grief reveal,
>   Not here the muse her virtues would relate.
>
> But wherefore weep? Her matchless spirit soars
>   Beyond where splendid shines the orb of day;
> And weeping angels lead her to those bowers
>   Where endless pleasures virtue's deeds repay.
>
> And shall presumptive mortals Heaven arraign,
>   And, madly, godlike Providence accuse?
> Ah, no! far fly from me attempts so vain:
>   I'll ne'er submission to my God refuse.
>
> Yet is remembrance of those virtues dear,
>   Yet fresh the memory of that beauteous face;
> Still they call forth my warm affection's tear,
>   Still in my heart retain their wonted place.

On Miss JESSY LEWARS, written by Robert Burns :—

> Say, sages, what's the charm on earth
>   Can turn Death's dart aside?
> It is not purity and worth,
>   Else Jessy had not died.

Westminster Abbey.   On GRACE SCOT :—

GRACE, eldest Daughter of Sir THOMAS MAULEVERER,
Of *Allerton, Mauleverer,* in *Yorkshire,* Baronet,
Born in the Year 1622, married to Col^{l.} THOMAS SCOT,
A Member of the Hon. House of Commons, in 1644,
And died the 24th of *Feb.* 1645,

> He that will give my Grace what is hers,
>   Must say that he hath not
>   Made only her dear Scot,
> But Virtue, Worth, and Sweetness, widowers.
>   Ex-Teris.

On a Friend, by the same, written in 1803 :—

> Oh friend! for ever loved, for ever dear!
> What fruitless tears have bathed thy honoured bier!
> What sighs re-echoed to thy parting breath,
> Whilst thou wast struggling in the pangs of death!
> Could tears retard the tyrant in his course;
> Could sighs avert his dart's relentless force;
> Could youth and virtue claim a short delay,
> Or beauty charm the spectre from his prey,—
> Thou still hadst lived to charm my aching sight,
> Thy comrade's honour, and thy friend's delight.
> If yet thy gentle spirit hover nigh
> The spot where now thy mouldering ashes lie,
> Here wilt thou read, recorded on my heart,
> A grief too deep to trust the sculptor's art.
> No marble marks thy couch of lowly sleep,
> But living statues there are seen to weep:
> Affliction's semblance bends not o'er thy tomb,
> Affliction's self deplores thy youthful doom.
> What though thy sire lament his failing line,
> A father's sorrows cannot equal mine!
> Though none like thee his dying hour will cheer,
> Yet other offspring soothe his anguish here:

But who with me shall hold thy former place?
Thine image, what new friendship can efface?
Ah, none! a father's tears will cease to flow;
Time will assuage an infant brother's woe;
To all, save one, is consolation known,
While solitary friendship sighs alone.

On a tombstone in the parish of *Closeburn, Scotland,* on JAMES HARCKNESS, who died 1733, aged 72 years:—

Below this stone his dust doth lie,
Who endured twenty-eight years' persecution by tyranny;
Did him pursue with hue and cry
Through many a lonesome place.
At last by Clavers he was ta'en—sentenced for to die.
But God, who for his soul took care,
Did him from prison bring;
Because no other cause they had,
But that he would not give up
With Christ his glorious King,
And swear allegiance to that beast,
The Duke of York, I mean.
In spite of all their hellish rage,
A natural death he died,
In full assurance of his rest
With Christ eternally.

In the parish of *Dunse*, near *Berwick*, the following may be seen:—

Beneath this stone three infants lie;
Say, are they lost or saved?
If death's by sin, they sinned, for they are here;
If heaven's by works, in heaven they can't appear.
Reverse the sacred page,—the knot's untied:
They die, for Adam sinned; they live, for Jesus died.

On MARY MEYNELL :—

> My beloved is gone down into his garden to gather lilies.
> SOLOMON'S SONG, chap. vi. verse 2.

Here lieth MARY, eldest child of FRANCIS MEYNELL, Esq., and CAROLINE STRACHAN, his wife, of *Brent-Moor, Devon*, who died *March* 27th, 1863, aged 4 years and 5 months.

My lovely little Lily, thou wert gathered very soon,
In the fresh and dewy morning, not in the glare of noon ;
The Saviour sent His angels to bear thee hence, my own,
And they'll plant thee in that garden where decay is never known.

From *Wilford* Church, near *Nottingham*, on a child aged 5 years :—

> As careful nurses they to bed do lay
> Their babes which would too long go wanton play,
> So, to prevent my youth's enticing crimes,
> Nature, my nurse, laid me to rest betimes.

In the Churchyard of *Weston Underwood*, in *Bucks*, on JAMES and HARRIETT SWANNELL, who died on the same day, aged 7 and 2 years :—

> I take these little lambs, said he,
>   And lay them on my breast :
> Protection they shall find in me,
>   In me be ever blest.
>
> Death can the bonds of life unclose,
>   But not dissolve my love ;
> Millions of infant souls compose
>   The family above.

Inscriptions on tombs in the Dissenters' Burial-place, near *Bunhill Fields:*—

In Memory of
Mr. JOHN GAME,
Who died the 15. 7mo 1711.
This stone is put up by
his loving Relict, in hope
of the first Resurrection to Glory.

REV. xx. 6.
Blessed and holy is he that hath part in the first Resurrection: on such the second Death hath no Power, but they shall be Priests of God and Christ, and shall reign with Him a Thousand Years.

Dame ELIZABETH FOCHE
(late Wife of Sir JOHN FOCHE),
Obiit XIII. *June*, MDCXCIII. *Ætatis Suæ* XXXII.

Here lyeth the Body of
Mrs. DORCAS BENTLEY,
the faithful, tender Wife
of JONATHAN BENTLEY, Citizen
and Coach-maker, of London;
Who lived much desired,
and dyed much lamented,
August the 3rd, 1693.

My Dear,
Thy zealous Care to serve thy God,
And constant Love to Husband dear,
Thy harmless heart to every one,
Remains still, tho' thy Corps lye here.
J. B.

Here lyeth
the Body of NICHOLAS LATIMER, Glover,
who departed this Life the
25th day of *April,* 1677,
and in the 70th Year of his Life.

He was poor Widows' Advocate,
And many pounds for them he gote,
Which he them gave without fail:
His loss therefore they much bewail.

Here lyeth the Body of
Mr. RICHARD FAIRCLOUGH, the worthy Son of the late
Reverend Divine, Mr. SAMUEL FAIRCLOUGH, of *Suffolk;*
Was sometime Fellow of *Emmanuel College,* in *Cambridge,*
afterwards Rector of *Mells,* in *Somersetshire.*
A Person, like his Father, eminent
For his natural Parts, acquired Learning and infused Grace:
Indued with a
most piercing Judgment, rich Fancy, and clear Expression;
And therefore
A good Expositor, a rare Orator, an excellent Preacher.
His Spirit and Temper was
Most Kind and Obliging,
Most Publick and Generous,
A great Contemner of Riches,
And Despiser of Vain-Glory;
Chearful, yet Watchful; Zealous, yet Prudent:
A pleasant Companion, and a most faithful Friend;
A pious Guide and Instructor,
By Doctrine and Example.
Obiit July 4, 1682. *Anno Ætat.* 61.

To the most deserving Memory of him and his Family,
This Monument was erected,
As a Testimony of Gratitude for many Obligations,
By Thomas Percivall, of the *Middle Temple*, Gent.
Anno Dom. 1682.

Here Lyeth the Body of Mrs. JANE PERCIVAL,
Who Dyed *March* the 10th.   In the Year 98.
Aged 52 Years.

Here lyeth the Body of ELIZABETH TWISLETON,
the Eldest Daughter of
the Right Honourable the Lord Viscount James Fynes,
Say and *Seale*,
Wife to John Twistleton, Esq., at *Dartford* in
Kent.   She dy'd on the 28th Day of
March, Anno Dom. 1673.

Here Lyeth the Body of
JOHN PENNYMAN, who was requir'd [by Abraham's God]
to offer up (as Abraham did)
An unusual Sacrifice at the *Royal Exchange*,
in *London*, upon the 28th
Day of *July*, 1670.   (An Account
of which he then caused to be
Printed, and hath ordered it to
be Reprinted in the Book of his Life.)
And for a perpetual Memorial
of which he order'd this Inscription to be set in
this Place.   He departed this Life
the 2nd day of *July*, 1706,
in the 78th Year of his Age.

Here resteth in Hope the Body of HANNAH, Wife
to NEHEMIAH BOURNE, Senior, sometime a Commander
at Sea and Commissioner for the Navy. By whom
he had 4 Sons and one Daughter.
Who after she had lived with him as a most
Affectionate Wife, above 52 Years, during which
Time she was a most suitable Companion to him in
various and extraordinary Paths of Divine
Providence by Sea and Land, at Home, and in
remote Parts, and an eminent Example and
Pattern to all that knew her, as well in the several
Excellences of a natural Temper, as those of the
Spiritual and Divine Life: being ripen'd for a
Better, she departed this World at *Ebisham* in
Surrey, upon the 10th of *June;* from thence was
brought to this Place, and buried the 21st, in the
Year of our Lord 1684, and of her Age 68.

LUCIA SMITH dyed *Octob.* the 6th, 1862, within a Day
of 12 years; who lived much beloved, and dyed greatly
lamented by all her Acquaintance; as not having known
her Equal for Natural Endowments at her Age.

EPITAPH.

Here lyes embalm'd in careful Parents' Tears,
A Virgin Branch, cropt in its tender Years:
Reader, as in a Glass, thou perfectly mayst see,
How all things here below vain and uncertain be.
Dear Virgin Child, Farewell! thy Mother's Tears
Cannot advance thy Memory (who wears
A Crown above the Stars); yet I must mourn,
And show the World mine Offerings at thy Urn.
'Tis not, Dear Child! a Stone can deck your Herse,
Nor can your Worth lodge in a narrow Verse.

No, no, blest Virgin! this engraven Breath
Is not to speak your Life, but weep your Death.
This Herse is only lay'd by th' careful Trust
Of a sad Mother, in Honour of your Dust.

EPITAPH.

Reader, pay thy Tribute here,
A Tear, a Rose, and then a Tear.
Grief may make thee Marble too,
Yet weep on, as Marbles do;
Gently let the Dust be spread
O'er a gentle Virgin's Head:
Press'd by no rude Passer by,
Nothing but a Mother's Eye.
Sacred Tomb, with whom we trust
Precious Piles of lovely Dust;
Keep them safely, sacred Tomb,
Till a Mother ask for Room.

Here lyeth the Body of

FRANCIS SMITH, Bookseller,

Who in his Youth was settled in a separate Congregation, where he sustained, between the years of 1659 and 1688, great Persecution by Imprisonments, Exile, and large Fines laid on Ministers and Meeting Houses, and for Printing and promoting Petitions for calling of a Parliament with several Things against Popery, and after near 40 Imprisonments he was fined 500*l.* for printing and selling the Speech of a Noble Peer, and Three Times suffered Corporeal Punishment. For the said Fine he was 5 years Prisoner in the *King's Bench*: his hard Duress there utterly impaired his Health. He dyed Housekeeper in the Custom-House, *December* the 22nd, 1691.

The Body of SAMUEL OKEY,
the Son of Samuel Okey, is here intomed:
He was born
Dec. the 11th, 1706, and dyed *July* the 4th, 1711.

> Here lyes, for ADAM'S first Offence,
> Beauty, Wit, and Innocence:
> E'er such another turns to Earth,
> Time shall throw a Dart at Death.

Near this Place lyeth interred
the Body of
LT.-COLL. WILLAM BLENNER HAYSELL,
who was a Lover of Arms,
and of Christian and *English* Liberties.
Obiit 6° *Jan.* 1699. *Ætate* 76.
In Hope of the Resurrection of the Just.

Here lyeth interred the Body of
ELIZABETH, Wife of EDMOND PORTMANS, of
Lond., Gent.,
Who dyed in the 70th Year of her Age, XBER. 22, 1693, and in the 45th Year of her Marriage; by whom he had 2 Sons and 5 Daughters: In Memory of whom, this Monument was by him erected, and in whom was that Question of SOLOMON's answered.
Prov. 31 & 10.

As also the Body of ELIZABETH, Eldest Daughter of
the said EDM. and ELIZABETH,
Who dyed in the 19th Year of her Age, *November* 12, 1669.

Here lyeth the Body of
Mr. ABEL COLLYER, Minister of the Gospel,
and Pastor of a Congregation at *Halsted*, in *Essex*,
who departed this Life the 29th Day of *May*, 1695,
in the 66th year of his Age.

He was for Self-Denial eminent;
To seek his Master's Glory fully bent:
In Gospel Truths of deep Insight;
Win Souls to Christ was his Delight:
Poor in Spirit, Rich in Faith,
Christ was his Wish, and Him he hath.

MORDECAI ABBOTT, Esq.,
Receiver-General Of His Majesty's Customs.
Obiit 29 *Feb.*, 1699. *Ætat.* 43.

Here ABBOTT, Virtue's great Example, lies,
The Charitable, Pious, Just, and Wise.
But how shall Fame, in this small Table, paint
The Husband, Father, Master, Friend, and Saint?
A Soul on Earth so ripe for Glory found,
So like to theirs who are with Glory crown'd,
That 'tis less strange such Worth so soon should go
To Heaven, than that it stay'd so long below.

JOHANNES ANTRUM.

Obiit 15 *Jan.*, 1704.

Behold thyself by me;
Such one was I as thou;
And thou in Time shalt be
Even Dust, as I am now.

Ætatis suæ 54.

Here lyes interred the Body of
Mr. THOMAS HOLMES,
Citizen and Haberdasher of *London*, and Son of Mr. Thomas Holmes, of *Wigson*, in the County of *Leicester*, who yielded to Nature the 4th Day of *December*, 1694, in the 38th Year of his Age.

    Dear HOLMES hath found
    A Home amongst the Blest,
    His wearied body for to rest :
    For nowhere can his Flesh
      True Slumber have ;
But in this Trust Home on Homely Grave,
His Soul in Heavenly Tunes doth sing,
    Hell, where's thy Triumph?
    Death, where is thy sting?

Here lyeth interred the Body of
Mr. JOHN GAMMON,
late Minister of the Gospel.
He departed this Life the 8th Day of *August*, 1699,
In the 47th year of his Age.

At the foot of the stone :—

This is the Foot-stone of
Mr. JOHN GAMMON,
Minister of the Gospel.

    Though dead I lye,
      I speak to you that live :
    Your Heart, your All,
      To Christ be sure to give.

Here they laid MARY THOMAS,
when Death snatched her from her Husband,
Ben. Thomas,

> Her Name, both Maid and Wife,
> And his the same throughout his Life.

Deceased the 22nd of *Nov.*, 1711.
Aged 35.

Here lyeth the Body
Of Mrs. HANNAH SYLVESTER,
Who left this Life, *April* the XII.,
A.D. MDCCI., aged LVII. Years.
Who lived in faithful and endearing Wedlock
XXX Years with Mr. Matt. Sylvester, too unworthy
of so great and meet an Help and Blessing.

> Flens veni in terras: sperans discedo, fuitque
> Vita mihi Christus; qui mihi vita manet:
> Pallida mors rapuit animam, subduxit & artus;
> Pars potior cœlo est reddita; corpus humo.

Here lyes the Body of
ANN JOHNSON,
Who liv'd Religiously, and dyed Piously,
The 4th of *January*, 169⅘,
In the 14th Year of her Age.

> The Body's here, the Soul is fled
>   To Regions which are pure and bright,
> And tho' the meaner Part lies dead,
>   The noblest's gone to Heavenly Light.

She did request that she might be
To her blest Saviour's Bosom ta'en,
And now she dwells where she doth see,
What does exceed Reports of Fame.

Here lies interred the Body of
Mr. EDWARD BAGSHAW,
Minister of the Gospel, who received from God
Faith to embrace it,
Courage to defend it,
and Patience to suffer for it,
When by the most despised, and by many persecuted;
Esteeming the Advantages of Birth, and Education, and
Learning (all eminent in him), as Things of Worth,
to be accounted Loss for the Knowledge
of Christ.
From the Reproaches of professed Adversaries,
He
took Sanctuary,
by the Will of God,
in
Eternal Rest,
the 28th of *December*,
1671.

Here also lyes the Body of
Mrs. MARGARET, late Wife of Mr. EDW. BAGSHAW,
who departed this Life the 20th of *February*,
1692.

Here the Wicked cease from Troubling,
And here the Weary be at Rest;
Here the Prisoners rest together;
They hear not the voice of the Oppressor.

Here lyeth interred the Body of that
Faithful Minister of Christ,
BENJAMIN HOLME,
who went to his Rest, *October* the Fifth, 1691,
in the Twenty-fourth year of his Age.

To the Memory of
LIEUT.-COLL. WILLIAM STYLE,
Late Citizen and Leatherseller of *London*.
A Man from his Youth devout toward God, and Pious to
his Parents;
Singularly just, industrious, and Diligent;
Second to none in Courage; Kind to his Friends,
and Charitable to all:
Who on his Death-bed enjoyed plentifully the Conscience
and Joy of a Good Life.
Dyed 2 *March*,
1670.

Here lyeth interred the Body of
EDWARD TUCKER,
Late of *Weymouth*, in *Dorsetshire*, who (by his own
Prediction) departed this Life,
March the 4th, 1700.

Here lyeth the Body of MRS. ANNE KNOLLEYS,
Daughter of John —eney, Esq., and Wife
of Hanseld Knollys (Minister of the Gospel),
by whom he had Issue 7 Sons and 3 Daughters;
who dyed *April* 30th, 1671, and in the 63rd
year of her Age.

> My only Wife, that in her Life
> Liv'd Forty Years with me,
> Lyes now in Rest, for ever blest
> With Immortality.
> My Dear is gone, left me alone,
> For Christ to do, and dye;
> Who did for me, and dy'd to be
> My Saviour God most High."

On the plank of an altar-monument of freestone, at the west :—

VAVASOR POWELL, a successful Teacher of the past, A sincere Witness of the present, and an useful Example to the future Age, lies interred, who in the Defection of so many, obtained Mercy to be found Faithful ; for which being called to several Prisons, he was there tried, and would not accept deliverance, expecting a better Resurrection : in hope of which he finished this Life and Testimony together, in the 11th year of his Imprisonment, and in the 53rd year of his Age, *October* 27, *An.* 1671.

> In vain Oppressors do themselves perplex
> To find out Arts how they the Saints may vex:
> Death spoils their Plots, and sets the Oppressed free;
> Thus VAVASOR obtains true Liberty.
> Christ him released, and now he's joyned among
> The martyred Souls, with whom he cries, "How long?"
> REV. vi. 10.

Here lyeth the Body of JOHN DENT, Son of John and Ann Dent, who died *April* the 5th, 1710, aged One year and a Half and Six Months.

After a short but sharp Affliction here,
I take my Leave of you, my Parents dear.
Low here I lye, in this soft Bed of Dust,
Waiting the Resurrection of the Just.
I, Phœnix-like, have my first Rising known,
And on the Wings of Love am upward flown:
My Heavenly Parts ascended up on high,
Whilst on Earth my Earthly Part doth . . .
'Till it shall rise again in Glory blest,
With all the Saints, in their eternal Rest.
My Parents dear, my Time was short, you see:
So live and die, that you may rest with me.

Here lyeth interred the Body of the
Reverend and Learned Divine,
Mr. ANTHONY FIDOE, who, till the Year 1660, was a
Fellow of *Trinity College*, in *Cambridge;*
but soon after (his conscience not permitting him to comply
with the Act commonly known by the Name
of *The Bartholomew Act*), he
resigned, not only his Fellowship, but a considerable
Living he was then in Possession of, in the
County of *Cambridge;* and since that time has continued
a Minister of the Gospel in several parts
of *England;* but for the last Thirty Years of his
Life, in the City of *London*.
He dyed a Bachelor, on the 17th day of *January*, 1715.
Aged 75 years.

Here lyeth GRACE, the only Daughter
of Thomas Cloudley, of *Leeds*, in the County of York,
who was first married to Peter Jackson, of *Leeds*,
To whom she bare 3 Sons and 2 Daughters.

Afterwards married to John Dickonson, of *London*, to whom she bare 1 Daughter, of which she dyed, 15th *February*, 1688, in the 31st Year of her Age.

> GRACE was her Name, and Grace she had;
> But now GRACE is with Glory clad.

Memento Mori.
Here lyes interr'd the Body of
MARY LILBURN,
the Wife of Nathaniel Lilburn, of *Cripplegate* Parish, who departed this Life *Nov.* 12th, 1713,
Aged 38.

> So here she lyes interr'd, who humbly gave
> Her Soul to God, her Body to the Grave.
> Throughout her Passage to a better Life,
> She prov'd a pious, virtuous, loving Wife.
> She dy'd to live, and humbly liv'd to dye;
> So God remov'd her to compleat her Joy:
> And her surviving Spouse in Christ doth trust
> To mix his Ashes with her sacred Dust."

Here Lyeth the Body of Mr. NATH. VINCENT,
Minister of the Gospel,
Who departed this Life *June* 22nd, 1697,
in the 59th year of his Age,
In Hopes of a Blessed and Glorious Resurrrection unto Eternal Life.

> Though dead I lie, I speak to you that live;
> Your Heart, your All, be sure to God you give:
> At Death the Day of Grace will fully end;
> In Grief for Bad, in Good Works your Time spend.
> Earth is Vanity; Christ's Worth, and of His Cross,
> The Virtue Know, and Greatness of Soul's Loss.
> Immortal Souls to benefit and save,
> I have thus made a Pulpit of my Grave.

A writer in the *Church and State Gazette*, in 1850, read the following inscription in a village churchyard, "beneath the shadow of a building wherein one of the holiest and bravest of our Martyrs spoke in eloquent simplicity":—

Stop, traveller: cast an eye, where this ground I under lie,
An accident once happened to me, which I hope may never happen to thee.

In *Hove* Churchyard, near *Brighton*:—

> Yes, thou art fled, and saints a welcome sing.
> Thine angel spirit soar'd on angel wing:
> Our blind affection might have ask'd thy stay;
> The voice of God hath call'd His child away.
> Like Samuel, early in the temple found,
> Sweet Rose of Sharon, plant of heavenly ground:
> Oh! more than Samuel bless'd, to thee was given,
> The God he served on earth, to serve in heaven.

At *Wickham-Market, Suffolk*:—

SARAH CULLAM, died *May* 3rd, 1805, aged 6 years.

> And now the lamp of life will burn no more,
> Her pitying neighbour does her loss deplore.
> Her parents' pride, now mourning o'er her bier,
> In fond regret they shed the heartfelt tear.
> They feel the loss, yet own the chast'ning rod,
> And yield in grief their daughter to her God.

At *St. Lawrence's, York*:—

To the memory of 4 Sons and 2 Daughters of JOHN and ANN RIGG, who were drowned in the River Ouse together, *August* 19th, 1830.

> Mark the brief story of a summer's day!
> At noon, Youth, Health, and Beauty launch'd away;
> Ere eve, Death wreck'd the bark, and quench'd their light,
> Their Parents' home was desolate at night;

Each pass'd alone that gulf no eye can see;
They met next moment in Eternity.
Friend! kinsman! stranger! dost thou ask me, Where?
Seek God's right hand, and hope to find them there.

On an infant:—

Thou lovely babe, Christ is thy rest:
Thy Saviour call'd thee to be blest.
Thou favour'd child, thy toils are o'er;
Thy soul's with Christ, to part no more.

Sacred to the memory of the Rev. RALPH TYRER, Vicar of *Kendal*, who died A.D. 1627:—

London bred me—Westminster fed me,
Cambridge sped me—My sister wed me,
Study taught me—Living sought me,
Learning brought me—Kendal caught me,
Labour press'd me—Sickness distress'd me,
Death oppress'd me—The Grave possess'd me,
God first gave me—Christ did save me,
Earth did crave me—And heaven would have me.

At *Cork*:—

RICHARD BOARDMAN,
Departed this life *October* 4th, 1782,
Ætatis 44.

Beneath this stone the dust of BOARDMAN lies,
His precious soul has soar'd above the skies;
With eloquence divine, he preach'd the word
To multitudes, and turn'd them to the Lord.
His bright example strengthen'd what he taught,
And devils trembled when for Christ he fought.
With truly Christian zeal he nations fired,
And all who knew him mourn'd when he expired.

At *St. Mary's, Lambeth :—*

Near this place are the remains of
WILLIAM BACON,
of the Salt Office, *London*, Gent.,
Who was killed by thunder and lightning,
at his window, *July* 12, 1787,
Aged 34 years.

By touch ethereal in a moment slain,
He felt the power of death, but not the pain;
Swift as the lightning glanced, his spirit flew,
And bade the rough tempestuous world adieu.
Short was his passage to that peaceful shore,
Where storms annoy and dangers threat no more.

At *Sutton Coldfield, Warwickshire :—*

As a warning to female virtue,
And a humble monument to female chastity,
This stone marks the grave
Of MARY ASHFORD,
Who, in the 20th year of her age, having
Incautiously repaired to a scene of amusement
Without proper protection,
Was shamefully ill-used and murdered,
On the 27th of *May*, 1817.

Lovely and chaste as is the primrose pale,
Rifled of sweetness by the passing gale :
MARY, the wretch who thee remorseless slew,
Avenging death, which sleeps not, will pursue ;
What though the deeds of blood be veil'd in night,
Shall not the Judge of all the earth do right ?
Fair, blighted flower ! the muse that mourns thy doom,
Rears o'er thy murder'd form this warning tomb.

At *Great Billing, Northamptonshire :—*

> JUSTINIAN BRASSGIRDLE underneath this stone
> Hath left his pawne of resurrection;
> Who four and fifty winters did afforde
> This flocke the pasture of God's heavenly worde,
> And all his lifetime did employ his care
> So to growe rich to make the poore his heyre.
> Being charitye's faithful steward, he imparts
> Twelve hundred pounds to nourish Oxford artes;
> Then if our God to them ope heaven doore,
> That give but drops of water to the poore,
> Sure his wise soul laid up a treasure there,
> That nere shall rust—who now bought heaven so deare;
> When faith and good workes have so long contended,
> That faith is almost dead, and good workes ended.
>
> *Obijt Octob.* 25, 1625.

At *Newington,* in *Surrey :—*

MATILDA BOWEN, died 12th *July*, 1799, aged 5 years and 8 months.

> Here rests in peace the body of a child,
> Who was in temper lovely, meek, and mild,
> In whom her parents greatly did delight,
> And she was precious in the Saviour's sight.
> As Death approach'd, she anxious was to fly
> To Jesus' breast, to dwell with Him on high:
> With outstretch'd arms, her father she address'd,
> "What is't o'clock?" she said with lab'ring breast.
> "Take me, take me, that I may be at rest."
> These were the last sweet words that she express'd.
> The Saviour heard, and caught her to the skies,
> And now she chaunts His praises in eternal joys.

In *Swallowfield* Churchyard :—

> Here lies a fair blossom mould'ring to dust,
> Ascending to heaven, to dwell with the just:

At *Bury St. Edmund's* :—

I. H. S.
Here lies interred the Body of
MARY HASELTON,
A young Maiden of this Town,
Born of Roman Catholic Parents,
And virtuously brought up,
Who, being in the act of Prayer,
Repeating her Vespers,
Was instantaneously killed by a flash
of lightning, *August* 16, 1785,
Aged 9 years.

Not Siloam's ruinous tower the victims slew
Because above the many sinn'd the few.
Nor here the fated lightning wreak'd its rage,
By Vengeance sent, for crimes matured by age;
For whilst the Thunder's awful voice was heard,
The little suppliant, with its hands uprear'd,
Address'd her God in prayers the Priest had taught,
His mercy craved, and His protection sought.
Learn, Reader! hence that Wisdom to adore
Thou canst not scan, and fear his boundless Power:
Safe shalt thou be, if thou perform'st His will,
Blest if He spares, and more blest should He kill.

At *Ely* Cathedral :—

MARIA SCOTT, died *April*, 1836, aged 7.

The cup of life just with her lips she prest,
Found the taste bitter, and declined the rest.
Averse: then turning from the face of day,
She softly sigh'd her little soul away.

At *Brandeston, Suffolk* :—

SOPHIA OLIVE PICKERING, died *March* 25, 1816.

> Loved infant, on this hill you rest
> Till rising higher to be blest.
> Oh, angel sweet, thy spirit's flown,
> Invited to thy Maker's throne.
> Escaped the bitter ills below,
> Secure from pain and mortal woe,
> Thy gentle soul celestial lives;
> In seraph strain now grateful gives
> Eternal praise to God on high,
> Who rules alike the earth and sky;
> Removed from keen affliction's rod,
> Thy biding place the breast of God.

This tablet her father erects to her dear memory.

At *St. Edmund's, Salisbury*, in memory of three children of JOSEPH and ARABELLA MATON, who died in their infancy, 1770:—

1

> Innocence Embellishes Divinely Complete,
> To Prescience Coegent Now Sublimely Great
> To the Benign, Perfecting, Vivifying State.

2

> So Heavenly Guardian Occupy the Skies,
> The Pre-existent God, Omnipotent, Allwise;
> He can Surpassingly immortalize thy Theme,
> And Permanent thy songul Celestial Supreme.

3

> When Gracious Refulgence bids the Grave Resign,
> The Creator's Nursing Protection be Thine:
> Thus each perspiring Æther will Joyfully Rise
> Transcendently Good, Supereminently Wise.

At *Wickham-Market:*—

CHARLES ELDRED, an excise officer, killed *Oct.* 18, 1848, aged 21.

> An accident his youthful life did end,
> No time allow'd His soul to recommend
> Unto that God who gave him his first breath,
> So suddenly his eyes were closed in death.

In the Churchyard of *St. George's-in-the-East, London:*—

Sacred
to the Memory of
MR. TIMOTHY MARR,
aged 24 years.
Also, MRS. CELIA MARR,
aged 24 years.
And their son, TIMOTHY MARR,
aged 3 months.
All of whom were most inhumanly murdered
in their dwelling house,
No. 29, *Ratcliff Highway, Dec.* 8, 1811.

> Stop, mortal, stop, as you pass by,
> And view this grave wherein do lie
> A father, mother, and a son,
> Whose earthly course was shortly run.
> For, lo! all in one fatal hour,
> O'ercome were they with ruthless power,
> And murder'd in a cruel state,
> Yea, far too horrid to relate,
> They spared not one to tell the tale,
> One for the other could not wail;
> The other's fate they never sigh'd,
> Loving they lived, together died.

> Reflect, O reader, on thy fate,
> And turn from sin before too late;
> Life is uncertain in this world,
> Oft in a moment we are hurl'd
> To endless bliss or endless pain,
> So let not sin within you reign.

In *Westbury* Churchyard :—

> The child was drown'd that's buried here,
> Dear reader! stop, and drop a tear;
> Not for the babe, but for its mother,
> Because she is left without another.
> To the will of God I must resign,
> In heaven I hope my babe to join.

At *Laxfield, Suffolk.* On a boy aged 10 years :—

> Sweet innocency's form lies here
> Lamented by its parents dear.
> They hope again in endless joy
> To meet again their lovely boy.

At *Norwich.* On JONATHAN LEWES, who died through a fall from his horse, *April* 7th, 1804, aged 32 years :—

> Judge me not, reader ; Christ is judge of all :
> I fell—stand'st thou? take warning by my fall;
> Be ready, lest thee sudden death surprise,
> And hence two witnesses against thee rise.

At *Hackney.* On MIRA HODGKINS, who died *Oct.* 3, 1803, aged 9 years :—

> Dearer than daughter, parallel'd by few,
> In sweetness, patience, suffering, —— adieu!
> Adieu! my MIRA, till that day more blest,
> When, if deserving, I with thee shall rest.

Come, then thy sire will cry in joyful strain,—
Oh! come to my paternal arms again.

At a village in *Shropshire*. On an infant:—

Here sweetly sleep awhile, blest babe; thy sun
In haste hath set, thy race of suffering done:
A stranger to thy great Creator's name—
Unknown to thee thy glorious Saviour's fame.
Nor fame, nor hope, nor love, nor other grace
Within thy infant bosom held their place.
No power hadst thou to shed one contrite tear,
One duteous act perform, or lisp one prayer.
But not in vain thy life! Thou hast not sown,
Yet the rich harvest reapest as thy own:
Thou hast not fought, but thou hast won the prize,
Hast never borne the cross, yet gain'd the skies.
E'en guilt was thine, as Adam's guilty race;
Yet such the Father's love—the Saviour's grace,
That Father's love hath turn'd thy night to day,
That Saviour's blood hath wash'd thy guilt away;
Clothed in His robe of righteousness divine,
Peace, pardon, life, and endless joys are thine.

At *Stanford, Notts:*—

Here lies the body of FRANCIS, the son of Mr. FRANCIS THWAITS, Rector of *Stanford*, and of ANN his Wife, who dyed the 4th *September*, in the 2nd year of his age, 1700.

As careful nurses
To their bed doe lay,
Their children which too
Long would wanton play;
So to prevent all my
Evening crimes,
Nature, my nurse, laid
Me to bed betimes.

At *Willesden* :—

WILLIAM ROBINSON, aged 2,
And
SALLY ROBINSON, aged 4,
Children of
WILLIAM ROBINSON, of the *Inner Temple*,
London, Gt.,
And ANNE, his Wife,
Anno Dom. 1750.
Fled from scenes of guilt and misery,
Without partaking of them;
And their bodies sleep in this monument,
United by mutual tenderness.
Their sympathising souls, impatient
of a separation,
And eager to rejoin their kindred angels,
With a smile took leave of their
weeping parents here,
And together ascended to their im-
mortal Sire above,
To sit at His right hand,
To be cherished in His paternal bosom,
To enjoy ineffable happiness,
And part no more;
These reflections, inspired by heaven;
Have taught their otherwise inconso-
lable parents to dry up their tears,
And yield a perfect resignation to the
Divine will,
Insomuch that they congratulate the
dear deceased

on their timely departure,
And mourn only for the living.

At *Wortham, Suffolk:*—

To the memory of a first grandchild,
MARION EDITH COBBOLD, *Jan.* 15, 1851.

She lived a treasure dearly prized,
In Jesus' name she was baptized.
When Jesus shall to judgment come,
We all shall find our heavenly home.

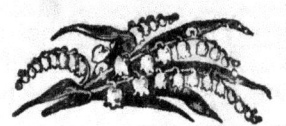

II.

Professional Epitaphs.

At *Bridgeford-on-the-Hill, Notts:*—

Sacred to the Memory of JOHN WALKER, the only son of BENJAMIN and ANN WALKER, Engineer and Pallisade Maker, died *September 22nd*, 1832, aged 36 years.

> Farewell, my wife and father dear;
> My glass is run, my work is done,
> And now my head lies quiet here.
> That many an engine I've set up,
> And got great praise from men,
> I made them work on British ground,
> And on the roaring seas;
> My engine's stopp'd, my valves are bad,
> And lies so deep within;
> No engineer could there be found
> To put me new ones in.
> But Jesus Christ converted me,
> And took me up above.
> I hope once more to meet once more,
> And sing redeeming love.

Inscription on the monument in *St. Margaret's Church, Westminster,* in remembrance of England's mighty benefactor, *The First English Printer* :—

To the memory of WILLIAM CAXTON, who first introduced into Great Britain the art of Printing, and who, A.D. 1477, or earlier, exercised that art in the Abbey of Westminster. This Tablet in remembrance of one to whom the literature of the country is so largely indebted, was raised A.D. MDCCCXX., by the Roxburgh Club, Earl Spencer, K.G., President.

The following on the celebrated printer and bookseller, JACOB TONSON, who died in 1735 :—

The volume of his life being finished, here is the end of JACOB TONSON. Weep, Authors, and break your pens : your TONSON, effaced from the book, is no more ; but print this last inscription on this last page of death, for fear that, delivered to the press of the grave, he, the Editor, should want a Title. Here lies a bookseller, the leaf of his life being finished, awaiting a new edition, augmented and corrected.

Honest FRANKLIN *imitated this last,* and designed it for himself :—

The body of BENJAMIN FRANKLIN, printer, (like the cover of an old book, its contents torn out, and stript of its lettering and gilding,) lies here, food for worms ; yet the work itself shall not be lost, for it will appear once more in a new and more beautiful edition, corrected and amended by the author. (He was born *Jan. 6th,* 1706 ; died *April 17th,* 1790.)

After the death of this sturdy patriot and sagacious writer, the *following singular sentiment* was inscribed to his memory :—

BENJAMIN FRANKLIN, the * (star) of his profession; the type of honesty; the ! (admiration) of all; and although the ☞ (hand) of death has put a . (period) to his existence, each § (section) of his life is without ‖ (a parallel).

The *following was written by Fontaine* for one of the well-known family of printers, named GRYPHE. Our readers must bear in mind that *griffe* is *a claw* :—

Le grand griffe qui tout griffe	The great Clawer who claws all
A griffe le corps de Gryphe ;	Has clawed the body of Gryphe ;
Le corps de ce Gryphe : mais	The body of *this* Gryphe : but
Non le les : non, non, jamais !	Not all of them : no, no, never.

On a Printer :—

> Here lies a form ; place no imposing stone
>   To mark the bed where weary it is lain ;
> 'Tis matter dead !—its mission being done—
>   To be distributed to dust again.
>
> The body's but the type at best of man,
>   Whose impress is the spirit's deathless page ;
> Worn out, the type is thrown to "pye" again—
>   The impression lives through an eternal age.

Here is *another Typographical Epitaph* :—

On L. GEDGE, printer, died 1818. In the Churchyard of *Bury St. Edmund's*. Here rest the remains of L. GEDGE, printer. Like a worn-out character, he has returned to the Founder, hoping that he will be re-cast in a better and more perfect mould.

Epitaph on a Blacksmith :—

> Here *cool* the *ashes* of MULCIBER GRIM,
> Late of this Parish, *Blacksmith;*
> He was born in *Seacole* Lane, and bred at *Hammersmith.*
> From his youth upwards he was much addicted
> to *vices,* and was often guilty of *forgery.*
> Having some talents for *irony,*
> He therefore produced many *heats* in his neighbourhood,
> Which he usually increased by *blowing
> up the coals.*
> This rendered him so unpopular, that when he found
> it necessary to adopt *cooling* measures,
> His conduct was generally accompanied with a *hiss.*
> Though he sometimes proved a *warm* friend, yet, where
> his interest was concerned, he made it a constant
> rule to *strike while the iron was hot,* regardless of the
> injury he might do thereby;
> And when he had
> any matter of moment upon the *anvil,* he seldom failed
> to *turn it to his own advantage.*
> Among the numberless instances that might be given of
> the cruelty of his disposition, it need only
> be mentioned
> That he was the means of *hanging* many of the innocent
> family of the *Bells,*
> Under the idle pretence of keeping them
> from *jangling;*
> And put great numbers of the *hearts of steel* into
> the *hottest flames,*
> merely (as he declared) to *soften* the obduracy
> of their *tempers.*

At length, after passing a long life in the commission of
these *black actions*, his *fire* being exhausted,
and his *bellows* worn out,
He *filed* off to that place where only the *fervid ordeal* of
his own *forge* can be exceeded ;
Declaring with his last *puff*, that man is born to trouble
as the *sparks* fly upwards.

This Epitaph was written by the poet Hayley, on a Blacksmith, which may now be found in several churchyards, as at *Rochdale, Lancashire; Bothwell, Scotland; Carisbrooke; Feltham,* in *Sussex;* and at *Westham,* in *Essex:*—

My sledge and hammer lie declined,
My bellows-pipes have lost their wind,
My fire's extinct, my forge decay'd,
My vice is in the dust now laid ;
My coal is spent, my iron's gone,
My nails are drove, my work is done,
My fire-dried corpse here lies at rest,
My soul, smoke-like, soars to be blest.

In *Sleaford* Churchyard. On HENRY FOX, a weaver :—

Of tender *thread* this mortal *web* is made,
The *woof* and *warp* and *colours* early fade ;
When power divine awakes the sleeping dust,
He gives immortal *garments* to the just.

In *Stepney* Churchyard :—

Here lies Daniel Saul,
Spitalfields weaver—and that's all.

And a similar one, on a JOHN HALL, in *St. Dunstan's.*

In *Edinburgh* Churchyard :—

> Here lies the banes o' Tammy Messer,
> O tarry woo' he was a dresser,
> He had some faults and many merits,
> And died of drinking ardent spirits.

On a Letter Founder at *Oxford :*—

> Under this stone lies honest SYL,
> Who dy'd, tho' sore against his will ;
> Yet in his fame he shall survive,—
> Learning shall keep his name alive ;
> For he the parent was of letters,
> He *founded*, to confound his betters :
> Tho' what those letters should contain
> Did never once disturb his brain.
> Since therefore, reader, he is gone,
> Pray let him not be trod upon.

Hammersmith Church, *Middlesex*, on THOMAS WORLIDGE, painter, died *Sept.* 23*rd*, 1766.

> He who had art so near to nature brought,
> As e'en to give to shadows life and thought,
> Had yet, alas ! no art or power to save
> His own corporeal substance from the grave ;
> Yet tho' his mortal part inactive lies,
> Still Worlidge lives—for genius never dies.

In *All Saints'* Churchyard, *Newcastle :*—

> Here lies ROBERT WALLIS,
> Clerk of All Hallows,
> King of Good Fellows,
> And Maker of Bellows.
> He Bellows did make to the day of his death,
> But he that made Bellows could never make breath.

On CORNELIUS BARKER, an Architect :—

> Here lies one whose deserved fame
> Will not yet fade or die ;
> His knowing head, when we are dead,
> Shall live in memory.

In *Gateshead* Churchyard, *Durham*, is the following to the memory of the Architect of the Exchange and Guildhall :—

> Here lies ROBERT TROLLOPE,
> Who made your stones roll up.
> When Death took his soul up,
> His body fill'd this hole up.

On Sir JOHN VANBRUGH, Architect :—

> Lie *heavy* on him, earth, for he
> Laid many a *heavy* load on thee.

In *St. Paul's Cathedral* :—

> Underneath is buried Sir CHRISTOPHER WREN,
> The builder of this Church and City,
> Who lived about ninety years,
> Not to himself, but to the public good.
> Reader ! if thou seekest his monument, look around.
> He died, *Feb. 25th*, in the 91st year of his age.

In *Bullingham* Old Churchyard :—

> This humble stone is o'er a builder's bed.
> Tho' raised on high by fame, low lies his head.
> His rule and compass are now lock'd up in store.
> Others may build, but he will build no more.
> His house of clay so frail, could hold no longer—
> May he in heaven be tenant of a stronger !

On a Drunken Cobbler :—

> Enclosed within this narrow stall,
> Lies one who was a friend to *awl*.
> He saved bad *soles* from getting worse,
> But d——ned his own without remorse,
> And though a drunken life he passed,
> Yet saved *his sole*, by *mending at the last.*

On JOSEPH BLAKETT, Poet and Shoemaker, of *Seaham*. Ob. 1810, by Lord Byron :—

> Stranger! behold interr'd together
> The *souls* of learning and of leather.
> Poor Joe is gone, but left his *all*—
> You'll find his relics in a *stall.*
> His work was neat, and often found
> Well-stitched, and with *morocco* bound.
> Tread lightly—where the bard is laid
> We cannot mend the shoe he made ;
> Yet he is happy in his hole,
> With verse immortal as his sole.
> But still to business he held fast,
> And stuck to Phœbus to the last.
> Then who shall say so good a fellow
> Was only leather and prunella ?
> For character—he did not lack it,
> And if he did—'twere shame to *Black-it!*

At *St. Leonard, Foster Lane, City*, was the tomb of ROBERT TRAPS, Goldsmith, (who died in 1526,) with this epitaph :—

> When the Bells be merely roung,
> And the Masse devoutly soung,
> And the Meate merely eaten,
> Then sall Robert Trappes, his Wyffs, and
> His Children be forgotten.

At the *Abbey Church, Sherborne,* on THOMAS PURDUE, who died on 1*st September,* 1711, aged 90. It appears that Cardinal Wolsey presented the great bell to the Church, and in 1670 it was recast by Purdue. No record is preserved of the original legend on the bell, but the following inscription was placed upon it :—

> This bell was new cast by me, Thomas Purdue,
> October 20th, 1670.
> Gustavus Horne, Walter Pride, churchwardens.
> By Wolsey's gift I measure time for all :
> To mirth, to grief, to church I serve to call.

The Epitaph on PURDUE'S tomb :—

> Here lies
> The Bell Founder
> Honest and true,
> Till ye resurrection
> Named Purdue.

The following is to be found in the Churchyard of *Upton-on-Severn :*—

> Beneath this stone, in hope of Zion,
> Doth lie the landlord of the "Lion."
> His son keeps on the business still,
> Resign'd unto the Heavenly will.

On JOHN SCOTT, a Liverpool Brewer :—

> Poor John Scott lies buried here :
> Although he was both *hale* and *stout,*
> Death stretch'd him on this *bitter bier.*
> In another world he *hops* about.

On a Dyer :—

> Beneath this turf a man doth lie,
> Who dyed to live, and lived to die.

On a Dyer :—

> Here lies a man who dyed of wool great store,
> One day he died himself, and dyed no more.

On a Watchmaker, from *Lidford* Churchyard, *Devon* :—

> Here lies in Horizontal position, the outside *case*
> of GEORGE ROUTLEIGH, Watchmaker,
> Whose abilities in that line were an honour
> to his profession :
> Integrity was the *Main-spring*, and Prudence the
> *Regulator* of all the *actions* of his life :
> Humane, generous, and liberal, his *Hand* never *stopped*
> till he had relieved distress.
> So sincerely *Regulated* were all his *Movements*, that
> he never *went wrong*, except when *set a-going*
> by people who did not know his *Key* :
> Even then he was easily *set right* again.
> He had the art of
> disposing his *Time* so well, that his *hours*
> glided away in one continual *round* of Pleasure and
> Delight, till an unlucky *moment* put a *period*
> to his existence.
> He departed this Life, *November* 14th, 1802, aged 57.
> *Wound up* in hopes of his being taken in hand by his
> *Maker*, and of being thoroughly *cleaned, repaired*,
> and *set-a-going* in the world to come.

On a Card Maker :—

> His card is cut ; long days he shuffled through
> The game of life : he dealt as others do.
> Though he by honours tells not its amount,
> When the last trump is play'd, his tricks will count.

In *Aliscombe* Churchyard, *Devonshire* :—

Here lie the remains of JAMES PADY, *brickmaker*, late of this parish, in hopes that his *clay* will be *re-moulded* in a workmanlike manner, far superior to his former perishable materials.

> Keep death and judgment always in your *eye*,
> Or else the devil off with you will fly,
> And in his *kiln* with brimstone ever fry:
> If you neglect the narrow *road* to seek,
> Christ will reject you, like a *half-burnt brick !*

Westminster Abbey. On JAMES WATT. The following inscription is understood to have been written by Lord Brougham :—

> Not to perpetuate a name
> Which must endure while the peaceful arts flourish,
> But to show that mankind have learned to
> honour those who best deserve their gratitude,
> The King,
> His Ministers and many of the Nobles and Commons of
> the Realm, raised this Monument to
> JAMES WATT,
> Who, directing the force of an original Genius, early
> Exercised in philosophic research, to the improvement
> of the Steam Engine,
> Enlarged the resources of his country, increased
> the power of man, and rose to an eminent place
> Among the most illustrious followers of Science and the
> real benefactors of the World.
> Born at *Greenock*, 1736.
> Died at *Heathfield*, in Staffordshire, 1819.

On an Undertaker :—

> Here lies ROB MASTER. Faith! 'twas very hard
>   To take away an honest Robin's breath ;
> Yet surely Robin was full well prepared,
>   For he was always looking out for *death*.

On a Pin Maker :—

> Here lies WILL. SHARPLESS. Oh, most cruel Death!
> Why didst thou rob WILL. SHARPLESS of his breath?
> He, in his lifetime, scraping one poor pin,
> Made better dust than thou canst make of him.

On a Baker :—

> Here lies DICK, a baker by trade,
>   Who was always in business praised ;
> And here snug he lies, in his oven, 'tis said,
>   In hopes that his bread may be raised.

In *Bromsgrove* Churchyard, *Worcestershire*, on a Railway Engineer, dated 1840 :—

> My engine now is cold and still,
> No water does my boiler fill ;
> My coke affords its flame no more ;
> My days of usefulness are o'er ;
> My wheels deny their noted speed,
> No more my guiding hand they need :
> My whistle, too, has lost its tone,
> Its shrill and thrilling sounds are gone ;
> My valves are now thrown open wide ;
> My flanges all refuse to guide,
> My clacks also, though once so strong,
> Refuse to aid the busy throng :
> No more I feel each urging breath ;
> My steam is now condensed in death.

Life's railway o'er, each station's passed,
In death I'm stopped, and rest at last.
Farewell, dear friends; and cease to weep:
In Christ I'm safe; in Him I sleep.

Wandsworth, Surrey. On HENRY SMYTH, Esq.:—

Here lyeth the Body of
HENRY SMYTH, Esq.,
Sometime Citizen and Alderman of *London,*
Who departed this Life the 3rd day of *January,*
An. Dom: 1627,
Being then neere the Age of 79 years.
Who, while he lived,
Gave unto the several Towns in Surrey, following,
One Thousand Pounds apiece,
To buy Lands for Perpetuity, for the Reliefe and setting
the poor People a worke in the said Townes, viz.:
To the Towne of Croydon, One Thousand Pounds;
To the Towne of Kingston, One Thousand Pounds;
To the Towne of Guildford, One Thousand Pounds;
To the Towne of Darkin, One Thousand Pounds;
To the Towne of Farnham, One Thousand Pounds;
And by his last Will and Testament did further Give and
Devise, to buy Lands for a Perpetuity for the
Reliefe and setting their Poor a worke,
Unto the Towne of Rygate, One Thousand Pounds;
Unto the Towne of Richmond, One Especyaltye, or Debt
of a Thousand Pounds;
And unto this Towne of Wandsworth (wherein he was
borne), the sume of Five Hundred Pounds,
For the same uses as before.
And did further Will and Bequeathe One Thousand

Pounds, to buy Lands for Perpetuity, to redeem poor
Captives and Prisoners from the Turkish Tyrannie; and
  not here stinting his Charity and Bounty,
    Did also Give and Bequeathe
The most part of his Estate (being to a great value) for
  the purchase of Lands of Inheritance for ever,
For the Reliefe of the Poor, and setting them a worke.
A pattern worthy of Imitation by those whom God hath
 blessed with the abundance of the Goods of this
    Life, to follow him herein.

On an old woman who kept a pottery shop in *Chester*:—

> Beneath this stone lies old KATHERINE GRAY,
> Changed from a busy life to lifeless clay,
> By earth and clay she got her pelf,
> But now is turn'd to earth herself.
> Ye weeping friends, let me advise,
> Abate your grief, and dry your eyes;
> For what avails a flood of tears?
> Who knows but in a run of years,
> In some tall pitcher or bread pan,
> She in her shop may be again?

In *Morville* Churchyard, near *Bridgenorth*, on JOHN CHARLTON, Esq., who was for many years Master of the Wheatland Foxhounds, and died *January* 20th, 1843, aged 63 years, regretted by all who knew him:—

> Of this world's pleasures I have had my share,
> And few the sorrows I was doom'd to bear.
> How oft have I enjoy'd the noble chase
> Of hounds and foxes striving for the race!
> But hark! the knell of death calls me away,
> So sportsmen, all, farewell! I must obey.

PROFESSIONAL EPITAPHS.

In *Arbroath* Churchyard :—

Here lies ALEXANDER PETER, *present* Town Treasurer of *Arbroath*, who died the 12th *January*, 1630.

> Such a treasurer was not since, nor yet before ;
> For common work " calsais trigs and schoir,"
> Of all others he did excell.
> He devised our skeol, and he hung our bell.

On PETER ARETINE :—

> Here ARETINE interr'd doth lie,
>   Whose satire lash'd both high and low ;
> His God alone it spared ; and why?
>   His God, he said, he did not know.

In All Saints' Church, *Hertford.* On Mr. WAKE :—

> Here *sleeps* Mr. *Wake*,
> Who gave the four small bells.

On a celebrated Cook :—

> Peace to his hashes.

Mitcham Church, *Surrey*. In the chancel is a monument to the memory of Sir AMBROSE CROWLEY, Alderman of *London*, who died in 1713, and is celebrated in No. 73 of the *Tatler*, under the name of Sir Humphrey Greenfat.

On a Parish Clerk :—

> Here lies within this tomb, so calm,
>   Old GILES—pray sound his knell—
> Who thought no song was like a psalm,
>   No music like a bell.

PROFESSIONAL EPITAPHS.

On FRANK RAID :—

>   Here lies the body of FRANK RAID,
>   Parish clerk, and gravestone cutter ;
>   And this is writ to lét you know,
>   What Frank for others used to do,
>   Is now for *Frank* done by another.

In *Crayford* Churchyard, *Kent* :—

Here lies the body of PETER ISUEL, thirty years Clerk of this parish. He lived respected, a pious and worthy man, and died on his way to Church to officiate at a wedding, on 31st *August*, 1811, aged 70. The inhabitants of *Crayford* raised this stone to his cheerful memory, and as a tribute to his faithful service :—

>   The life of this clerk was just threescore and ten,
>   Nearly half of which time he had sung out *Amen.*
>   In his youth he was married, like other young men;
>   But his wife died one day, so he chaunted *Amen.*
>   A *second* he took—she departed—what then?
>   He courted and married a third with *Amen.*
>   His joys and his sorrows were *treble*, but then
>   His voice was deep *bass*, as he sung out *Amen.*
>   The *horn* was exalted in blowing *Amen*,
>   He lost all his *wind* at threescore and ten ;
>   And here, with *three wives*, he waits till again
>   The trumpet shall rouse him to sing out *Amen.*

At *Weston* :—

>   Here lies entomb'd within this vault so dark,
>   A tailor, cloth-drawer, soldier, and parish clerk ;
>   Death snatch'd him hence, and also from him took
>   His needle, thimble, sword, and prayer-book.
>   He could not work, nor fight,—what then?
>   He left the world, and faintly cried, "Amen!"

On a Tailor and Barber :—

> In a timber surtout here are wrapt the remains
> Of a mower of beards and a user of skeins ;
> 'Twas the shears of grim Death cut his stay-tape of life,
> And press'd him away from twist, razors, and wife ;
> But the prayer of all people he sew'd for or shaved,
> Is that he's with the remnant of those that are saved.

From *Bolton-le-Moors* Churchyard :—

Sacred to the Memory of FREDERIC WEBB, Coach Proprietor, of the firm of Webb, Houlden, and Co., of *Bolton*, who departed this life the 9th *December*, 1825, aged twenty-three years. Not being able to combat the malevolence of his *enemies*, who sought his destruction, was taken prematurely from an affectionate loving wife and infant child, to deplore the loss of a good husband, whose worth was unknown, and who died *an honest man*.

Westminster Abbey. On Sir ANTHONY BURY GODFREY, Knt. :—

> Sir ANTHONY BURY GODFREY,
> who after being Knighted
> For his services to his King and Country,
> And discharging the Office of a Justice of the Peace,
> with unwearied assiduity and unwonted zeal,
> Was suddenly missed on the 12th of *October*, 1678,
> and after four days was found
> Barbarously and butcherly Murdered !
> *History will expose the rest.*

St. Michael's, *Cornhill*, City:—

> Hereunder lyeth a Man of Fame,
> WILLIAM WALWORTH, call'd by name;
> Fishmonger he was, in Lifetime here,
> And twice Lord Mayor, as in Bookes appeare:
> Who with courage stout, and manly might,
> Slew Wat Tyler, in King Richard's sight;
> For which act done, and trew intent,
> The King made him Knight incontinent,
> And gave him Armes, as here you see,
> To declare his Fact and Chivalrie.
> He left this life, the year of our God,
> Thirteen hundred, fourscore, and three odd.

At *Bunny, Notts*, in the chancel of the Church lies buried THOMAS PARKINS, the famous wrestler, and on a handsome marble monument he is represented in a wrestling attitude, and Time with his scythe mowing him down.

On WILLIAM WOOLLETT, the celebrated engraver:—

> Engraved by genius on the human heart,
>   WOOLLETT, thy works shall stand without a stain;
> And though the great original is gone,
>   The first impression ever shall remain.

The Philosopher of *Mantua*, POMPONAZZI, wrote his own epitaph:—

> Here I lie entomb'd; wherefore, I know not,
> Nor do I care whether *thou* knowest:
> If thou art well, it is well; while living, *I* was well,
> And mayhap I am well even now;
> But be it so or not, I cannot tell thee.

At *Highgate* Cemetery may be seen a monument erected to the memory of LILLYWHITE, the celebrated cricketer, and it has a significant emblem, being marked with a wicket upset by a ball.

On a Cricketer, in a Cemetery near *Salisbury* :—

>I bowl'd, I struck, I caught, I stopp'd—
>>Sure life's a game of cricket ;
>I block'd with care, with caution popp'd,
>>Yet Death has hit my wicket.

Some few years since, in the village Churchyard of *Leeds, Kent*, a stone was erected, with an inscription having blanks, which have since been filled up :—

In memory of JAMES BARHAM, of this parish, who departed this life *January* 14th, 1818, aged 93; and who from the year 1774 to the year 1804, rung in Kent and elsewhere 112 peals, not less than 5,040 changes in each peal, and called bobs, etc., for most of the peals ; and April 7th and 8th, 1761, assisted in ringing 40,320 bob-majors on Leeds bells in twenty-seven hours.

According to Strabo, the Greek geographer, the following epitaph was engraved upon the sepulchre of SARDANAPALUS :—

SARDANAPALUS, son of Anacyndaraxes, caused the towns of Anchiales and Tarsus to be built in one day. Pass on, stranger, eat, drink, and amuse thyself, for nought else is worth a fillip.

This unworthy philosophy has been commemorated in Byron's couplet :—

>Eat, drink, and sleep, what will the rest avail us?
>So said the royal sage, Sardanapalus.

Epitaph on the death of JOHN WARNER, late Lord Maior of the Citie of *London* :—

>Here lies my Lord Maior under this stone,
>That last Bartholomew-faire no Puppets would owne;
>But next Bartholomew-faire, who liveth to see,
>Shall view my Lord Maior, a puppet to bee,
>Which sight shall for ever continue his Fame,
>That he may dye never, but here have a Name.

Nov. 17th, 1648.   JOHN WARNER, Junior.

On a Linen Draper :—

>Cottons and Cambrics, all adieu,
> And muslins, too, farewell;
>Plain, striped, and figured, old and new,
> Three-quarters, yard, and ell;
>By nail and yard I've measured ye,
> As customers inclined;
>The church-*yard* now has measured me,
> And *nails* my coffin *bind*.

On a Woodman, at *Ockham, Surrey*, 1736 ;—

>The Lord saw good, I was lopping wood,
> And down fell from the tree;
>I met with a check, and broke my neck,
> And so death lopp'd off me.

On an Author :—

>A life of labour, by no pause relieved,
>Wore out a brain which splendid thoughts conceived.
>Had Fortune kindly given him more of leisure,
>The world, perhaps, had miss'd—he gain'd—a pleasure;
>With less of friction, and much more of rust,
>Death might have waited longer for his dust.

In the Church of *Walton-on-Thames, Surrey,* is the tomb of LILLEY, the Astrologer, with the following inscription :—

> Ne oblivione conteretur urna Gulielmi Lilii,
> Astrologi peritissimi qui fatis cessit vito
> idus Junii anno Christo Juliano MDCLXXXI.
> Hoc illi posuit amoris monumentum, Elias
> Ashmole Armiger.

Lyme Church, *Dorset.* On WILLIAM HEWLIN :—
Here lieth the body of WILLIAM HEWLIN, son of William Hewlin, Merchant, of *London,* and grandson of William Hiffen, Esq., Alderman of *London,* who suffered martyrdom before he was full twenty years of age, for engaging with the Duke of Monmouth, for the Protestant religion and English liberty, against Popery and Slavery, *September* 17th, 1685.

In *Upsala* Cathedral, the finest ecclesiastical edifice in the kingdom of *Sweden,* lies interred under a stone near the main door, with his much-loved wife by his side, LINNÆUS, the pride of the place. The stone bears no inscription—not even his name; but at a short distance from it there is a bust of the great naturalist, cut in *alto-relievo* on black marble, and the following inscription engraved on a tablet of beautiful Swedish porphyry :—

> Botanicorum Principe,
> Amici et Discipuli.
> MDCCXCVIII.

Axbridge Church, *Somerset.* There is a fine old brass plate in the floor of the north aisle here, with the portraitures of a male and female kneeling, and the following inscription underneath :—

Here lie the remains of ROGER HARPER, formerly a merchant or trader of this town, and JOANNA his wife; which Roger indeed died on the twenty-second day of the month of *August*, and the said Joanna died on the same day in the preceding month, in the year of our Lord, MCCCCXCIII.

"May God be propitious to the souls of both."

HENRY WALTON, a statesman and author, who died in 1639, desired that on his tomb should be placed an inscription which he himself indited :—

Here lies he who composed this sentence—*The itch of contention is the plague of the Church!* Seek his name elsewhere!

On a Schoolmaster of the Parish, in the Churchyard of *Curry*, near *Edinburgh*, who died in 1696 :—

> Beneath thir stanes lie MEEKIE'S banes:
> O Satan! should you tak him,
> Appoint him tutor to your weans,
> And clever deils he'll mak them.

A similar one on a Schoolmaster, in *Cleish* Parish, *Fifeshire*, was written by Robert Burns.

In *Dunmore* Churchyard, *Ireland*:—

Here lie the remains of JOHN HALL, Grocer.
The world is not worth a *fig*, and I have good *raisins* for saying so.

At the Church of *East Hucknall, Derbyshire,* in memory of one of the Duke of Devonshire's park keepers :—

> My gun's discharged,
> My ball is gone,
> My powder's spent,
> My work is done.
> Those panting deer
> I've left behind
> May now have time
> To gain the wind,
> Since I, who oft have
> Chased them o'er
> The verdant plains,
> Am now no more.

A faithful servant, who died at the commencement of 1707, has to the description of his merits :—

Here lieth JOHN JAMES, the old cook of *Newby*, who was a faithful servant to his master, and an upright, downright honest man.

These uncomfortable lines added :—

> Banes among stanes, do lye so still,
> While the soul wanders e'en where God will.

On Dr. JOHNSON, by Soame Jenyns :—

> Here lies poor JOHNSON. Reader! have a care,
> Tread lightly, lest you rouse a sleeping bear.
> Religious, moral, gen'rous and humane,
> He was, but self-conceited, rude, and vain :
> Ill-bred, and overbearing in dispute,
> A scholar and a Christian, yet a brute.
> Would you know all his wisdom and his folly,
> His actions, sayings, mirth, and melancholy ;
> Boswell and Thrale, retailers of his wit,
> Will tell you how he wrote, and talked, and spit.

Carew, in his Survey of *Cornwall*, tells us that old age is very common, one person he mentions as living to the age of 130, another 112, and again 110. He made this epitath on a Cornish beggar :—

>Here Brawne, the quondam beggar lies,
>   Who counted by his tale
>Some sixscore winters and above,
>   Such virtue is in ale.
>Ale was his meat, his drink, his clothes,
>   Ale did his death reprieve :
>And could he still have drunk his ale,
>   He had been still alive.

To the Pie-House Memory of NELL BATCHELOR, the *Oxford* Pie-Woman :—

>Here, into the dust
>The mouldering crust
>Of ELEANOR BATCHELOR's shoven ;
>   Well versed in the arts
>   Of pies, custards, and tarts,
>And the lucrative skill of the oven.
>   When she'd lived long enough,
>   She made her last puff—
>A puff by her husband much praised.
>   Now here she doth lie,
>   And makes a dirt pie,
>In hopes that her crust shall be raised.

Epitaph on JOHN ADAMS, Carrier, of *Southwell, Notts*, by Lord Byron :—

>JOHN ADAMS lies here, of the parish of Southwell,
>A *carrier* who *carried* his can to his mouth well ;
>He *carried* so much, and he *carried* so fast,
>He could *carry* no more— so was *carried* at last ;
>For the liquor he drank, being too much for one,
>He could not *carry*-off,—so he's now *carri-on*.

On a Magistrate, who had formerly been a Barber :—

> Here lies Justice ; be this his truest praise :
> He wore the wig which once he made, and learnt
> to shave both ways.

CECIL CLAY, the counsellor of Lord Chesterfield, caused this whimsical pun upon his name to be put on his tombstone : two ciphers of C.C., and underneath—

> "Sum quod fui." (I am what I was.)

On THOMAS MAGINN, LL.D., at *Walton-on-Thames*, died *August* 20th, 1842, by J. G. Lockhart :—

> Here early to bed, lies kind THOMAS MAGINN,
> Who with genius, wit, learning, life's trophies to win,
> Had neither great lord nor rich cit of his kin,
> Nor discretion to set himself up as to tin ;
> So his portion soon spent, like the poor heir of Lynn,
> He turn'd author ere yet there was beard on his chin ;
> And whoever was out, or whoever was in,
> For your Tories his fine Irish brains he would spin ;
> Who received prose and rhyme with a promising grin,
> "Go a-head, you queer fish, and more pow'r to your fin !"
> But to save from starvation stirr'd never a pin.
> Light for long was his heart, tho' his breeches were thin,
> Else his acting, for certain, was equal to Quin :
> But at last he was beat, and sought help of the bin,
> (All the same to the doctor, from claret to gin !)
> Which led swiftly to gaol, with consumption therein.
> It was much, when the bones rattled loose in the skin,
> He got leave to die here, out of Babylon's din.
> Barring drink and the girls, I ne'er heard of a sin :—
> Many worse, better few, than bright, broken Maginn.

On a Lawyer :—

> See how God works His wonders now and then, —
> Here lies a lawyer and an honest man.

On Mr. STRANGE, a Lawyer :—

> Here lies an honest lawyer, that is STRANGE.

From the interior of *Chichester* Cathedral, on a Crier of Periwinkles :—

> Periwinks! Periwinkles! was ever her cry;
> She labour'd to live, poor and honest to die.
> At the last day again how her old eyes will twinkle!
> For no more will she cry Periwinks! Periwinkles! `
> Ye rich, to virtuous want regard pray give;
> Ye poor, by her example, learn to live.

Died *Jan.* 1, 1786, aged 77.

On MILLS, the Huntsman :—

> Here lies JOHN MILLS, who over hills
> Pursued the hounds with hallo;
> The leap though high, from earth to sky,
> The huntsman we must follow.

On WILLIAM PRYNNE :—

> Here lies the corpse of WILLIAM PRYNNE,
> A bencher late of Lincoln's Inn;
> Who rudely thrust thro' thick and thin,
> Was never out—nor never in.

> A shameless, graceless, gospel-spiller,
> An endless, restless, margin-filler;
> To King and Bishops no good willer,
> To Church and State a caterpillar.

> Against his fate in vain he shrugs,
> In hopes of life, himself he hugs;
> And whilst he for more tether tugs,
> Death crops the remnant of his lugs.

On a Quack :—

> I was a quack, and there are men who say
> That in my time I physick'd lives away;
> And that at length I by myself was slain
> By my own drugs, ta'en to relieve my pain.
> The truth is, being troubled with a cough,
> I like a fool consulted Dr. Gough,
> Who physick'd me to death, at his own will,
> Because he's licensed by the state to kill:
> Had I but wisely taken my own physic,
> I never should have died of cold and 'tisick.
> So all be warn'd, and when you catch a cold,
> Go to my son, by whom my medicine's sold.

On JUDGE BOAT, by Swift :—

> Here lies JUDGE BOAT within a coffin:
> Pray, gentle folks, forbear your scoffing.
> A *boat*, a *judge!* Yes, where's the blunder?
> A *wooden* judge is no such wonder!
> And in his robes you must agree,
> No boat was better *deckt* than he.
> 'Tis needless to describe him fuller;
> In short, he was an able *sculler.**

On the Driver of the Coach that ran between *Aylesbury* and *London*, by the Rev. H. Bullen, Vicar of Dunton, Bucks, in whose churchyard the man was buried :—

> PARKER, farewell! thy *journey* now is ended.
> Death has the *whip-hand*, and with dust is blended;
> Thy *way-bill* is examined, and I trust
> Thy last *account* may prove exact and just.
> When He who drives the chariot of the day,
> Where life is light, whose Word's the living way,
> Where travellers, like yourself, of every age,
> And every clime, have taken their last *stage*,
> The God of mercy, and the God of love,
> *Show you the road* to Paradise above!

* Probably the author meant *scholar*, and wilfully mistook.

On a Coroner who hanged himself :—
> He lived and died by suicide.

On Sir PHILIP SYDNEY :—
> England hath his body, for she it fed ;
> Netherlands his blood, in her defence shed ;
> The heavens have his soul,
>   The Arts have his fame,
> The soldier his grief,
>   The world his good name.

Epigrammatic Epitaph on a Dustman :—
> Beneath yon humble clod, at rest,
> Lies ANDREW, who if not the best,
>   Was not the very worst man :
> A little rakish, apt to roam,
> But not so now ; he's quite at home,
>   For ANDREW was a dustman.

In *East Bergholt* Church, *Suffolk* :—

Edward	EDWARD LAMBE,	Lambe
Ever	second sonne of	Lived
Envied	Thomas Lambe,	Laudably
Evill	of *Trimley*,	Lord
Endured	Esquire.	Lett
Extremities	All his days	Like
Even	he lived a Bachelor.	Life
Earnestly	Well learned in Deveyne	Learne
Expecting	and Common Lawes,	Ledede
Eternal	with his councell he	Livers
Ease	helped many, yett took	Lament
	fees scarse of any.	

He dyed the 19th *November*, 1647.

In *Arlington* Churchyard, *Devonshire* :—

> Here lies WILL BURGOIN, a squire by descent,
> Whose death in this world many people lament.
>   The rich for his love,
>   The poor for his alms,
>   The wise for his knowledge,
>   The sick for his balms.
> Grace he did love, and vice control ;
> Earth hath his body, and heaven his soul.
> The twelfth of August in the morn died he,
>   1   6   2 and 3.

There are many curious anecdotes in medical history relative to the sepulchral habitations and honours of medical men. Some have not chosen to be buried in churches or churchyards, fearing to encounter some of their former patients, and having over their heads inscribed :—

> At length a grave—spots for him provided,
> Where all through him so many of us die did.

VERHEYEN, professor of anatomy and physic, at *Louvain*, composed the following epitaph himself :—

PHILIP VERHEYEN, doctor and professor of physic, ordered his mortal part to be buried here, in the churchyard, that he might not pollute the church, and infect it with noxious effluvia.

This seems to have given a hint to a doctor in *Staffordshire*, who was buried in a garden, with this inscription :—

Here lieth Dr. —— who departed this life *December* 22, 1745, and desired to be interred here in his own garden, rather than in a churchyard, lest he who had studied to promote man's health while alive, should be detrimental to it when dead, as well as defile the house of God. Aged 66.

Epitaph on a Physician, Dr. CHARD :—

> Here lies the corpse of Dr. CHARD,
> Who fill'd the half of this churchyard.

Epitaph written by Dr. GODFREY, on himself. He died in *Dublin*, 1755 :—

> Epitaphium Chymicum.
> Here lieth to *digest, macerate,* and *amalgamate* with clay,
> In *Balneo Arenæ,*
> *Stratum super Stratum,*
> The *Residuum, Terra damnata* and *Caput Mortuum,*
> Of BOYLE GODFREY, Chymist and M.D.
> A man, who in this Earthly *Laboratory,* pursued various
> *Processes* to obtain *Arcanum Vitæ,*
> or the Secret to Live :
> Also, *Aurum Vitæ,*
> or, the art of getting rather than making Gold.
> *Alchymist*-like, all his Labour and *Projection,*
> as *Mercury* in the Fire, *Evaporated* in *Fume,* when he
> *Dissolved* to his first principles.
> He *departed* as poor
> as the last drops of an *Alembic;* for Riches are not
> poured on the *Adepts* of this world.
> Though fond of News, he carefully avoided the
> *Fermentation, Effervescence,* and *Decrepitation* of this life.
> Full seventy years his *Exalted Essence*

PROFESSIONAL EPITAPHS. 115

was *hermetically sealed* in its *Terrene Matrass;* but the
Radical Moisture being *exhausted,* the *Elixir Vitæ* spent,
And *exsiccated* to a *Cuticle,* he could not *suspend*
longer in his *Vehicle,* but *precipitated Gradatim, per
Campanam,* to his original dust.
May that light, brighter than *Bolognian Phosphorus,*
preserve him from the *Athanor, Empyreuma,* and *Reverberatory Furnace* of the other world,
Depurate him from the *Fæcas* and *Scoria* of this,
Highly *Rectify* and *Volatilize* his *æthereal* spirit,
Bring it over the *Helm* of the *Retort* of this Globe, place
it in a proper *Recipient* or *Crystalline* orb,
Among the elect of the *Flowers of Benjamin;* never
to be be *saturated* till the General *Resuscitation, Deflagration, Calcination,* and *Sublimation* of all things.

Salisbury Cathedral.   On Dr. D'AUBIGNY TUBERVILLE :—

M. S.
Near this place is interred
the most expert and successful Oculist that ever was,
perhaps that ever will be,
DOCTOR D'AUBIGNY TUBERVILLE,
Descended from two Families of those names, than which
there are few more Ancient or Noble.
During the Civil Wars he bore arms for the King. After
the Surrender of Exeter,
he lived at *Wayford* and *Crookham;* but those towns
not affording convenience to his numerous patients,
he removed to *London,*
intending to settle there; but not having his health, he

left it, and lived in *Salisbury* more than thirty years,
doing good to all, and being beloved by all.
His great fame caused multitudes to flock to him, not
only from all parts of this kingdom, but also from
Scotland, Ireland, France, and *America.*
He died *April* the 21st, 1696, in the 85th year of his age,
and left his estate betwixt his only sister and niece,
at whose expense this monument was erected.
Doctor Walter Pope
Wrote this Epitaph, to perpetuate his gratitude, and to the
memory of his Friend and Benefactor.

Mortlake, Surrey. On JOHN PARTRIDGE :—

JOHN PARTRIDGE,
Astrologer and Doctor of Physic,
Born at *East Sheen,* in the County of *Surrey,*
Died the 14th *June,* Anno 1715.
He was Physician to two Kings and one Queen, Charles
the 2nd, William the 3rd, and Queen Mary ;
He was created Doctor of Physic at Leyden, in Holland.

On Dr. MOUNSEY, Physician to Chelsea Hospital. He left his body to the Institution, and at one time intended it should be buried in his garden, with an epitaph written by himself in 1788 :—

> Here lie my old bones : my vexation now ends :
> I have lived much too long for myself and my friends.
> As to churches and churchyards, which man may call holy,
> 'Tis a rank piece of witchcraft, and founded in folly.
> What the next world may be, never troubled my pate ;
> And be what it may, I beseech you, O Fate !
> When the bodies of millions rise up in a riot,
> To let the old carcase of Mounsey be quiet.

On Dr. STAFFORD, a remarkably fat man :—

Take heed, O good traveller, and do not tread hard,
For here lies Dr. Stafford *in all this churchyard.*

In *Hendon* Churchyard, *Middlesex.* On THOMAS CROSSFIELD, M.D., written by himself :—

Beneath this stone TOM CROSSFIELD lies,
Who cares not now who laughs or cries;
He laugh'd when sober, and when mellow,
Was a *harum scarum* heedless fellow.
He gave to none design'd offence,
So *Honi soit qui mal y pense.*

At *Cardross*, in *Dumbartonshire*, Dr. TOBIAS GEORGE SMOLLETT, the well-known author of *Roderic Random*, and other works, was born, and adjacent to the place of his nativity has been erected a lofty column to his memory, with an elegant Latin inscription.

In St. John the Baptist Church, Savoy, *London*, is a monument erected in 1846, to the memory of Dr. CAMERON, the last person executed on account of the rebellion of 1745, with the following inscription :—

To the Memory of Dr. ARCHIBALD CAMERON, whose
remains after his Execution were deposited in
the Vault beneath,
This Monument, with the gracious permission of
Her Majesty the Queen Victoria,
is erected by his great-grandson, A.D. 1846,
One hundred years after the battle of Culloden.

To soothe the sufferer then was all thy thought,
  Whate'er the banner under which he fought.
Thy hand would staunch the blood of him that bled,
  Were it for Brunswick or for Stuart shed.

In *Stepney* Churchyard. On Captain JOHN DUNCH, who died 1697, aged 67 :—

Though Boreas' blasts and Neptune's waves
  Have toss'd me to and fro,
In spite of both, by God's decree,
  I anchor here below,
Where I do now at anchor ride
  With many of our fleet ;
Yet once again I must set sail,
  Our admiral, Christ, to meet.

All Saints', *Hertford.* On Captain WILLIAM MINORS :—

Here lieth the Body of
Captain WILLIAM MINORS,
Who, after Ten Voyages to the *East Indies,*
Departed this life the 18th day of *July,* 1667,
In the 74th year of his age,
And chose this place for his Harbour
Until the Resurrection.

From the Churchyard of *Barwick-in-Elmet, Yorkshire* :—

Here lies, retired from busy scenes,
A first lieutenant of Marines,
Who lately lived in gay content
On board the brave ship "Diligent."
Now stripp'd of all his warlike show,
And laid in box of elm below,
Confined in earth in narrow borders,
He rises not till further orders.

In *St. Brelade* Churchyard, *Jersey*. On an old sailor :—

 Weep for a seaman, honest and sincere,
 Not cast away, but brought to anchor here.
 Storms had o'erwhelm'd him, but the conscious wave
 Repented, and resign'd him to the grave.
 In harbour, safe from shipwreck now he lies.
 Till Time's last signal blazes through the skies,
 Refitted in a moment he'll then be,
 Sail from this port on an eternal sea.

In *Stoneham* Parish Church, *Hampshire* :—

D.O.M.

This Monument is sacred to the Memory of
EDWARD HAWKE,
Lord Hawke, Baron of Tawton, in the County of York,
Knight of the Bath,
Admiral and Commander-in-Chief of the Fleet ;
Vice-Admiral of Great Britain, etc., etc.
Who died *October* 17th, 1781,
Aged 76.
The bravery of his soul was equal to the dangers he
encountered ; the cautious intrepidity of his
deliberations superior even to the conquest
he obtained. The annals of his life compose
a period of naval glory unparalleled
in later times ; for wherever he
sailed, victory attended him.
A prince, unsolicited,
conferred on him
dignities he
disdained
to ask.

The last Epitaph may also be found in *Kilkeran* Churchyard, *Ayrshire*, where it commemorates a certain shipmaster, one JOHN FERGUSON, of *Ayr*.

A very similar one is at the parish Church of *Duffus*, in *Morayshire*.

Also in the Churchyard of St. Mary Key, *Ipswich* :—

Tho' Boreas' blasts and Neptune's waves have toss'd me to and fro,
Yet now at last, by Heaven's decree, I harbour here below,
Where at anchor I do lie with others of our fleet,
Till the last trump do raise us up our admiral, Christ, to meet.

In the west part of *Fife*, in the churchyard of the village of *Torryburn*, part of an Epitaph remains which deserves notice. A portion was very absurdly erased by the owner of the burying ground, to make room for the names of some of his kindred. The whole epitaph formerly stood thus :—

> At anchor now, in Death's dark road,
>   Rides honest Captain HILL,
> Who served his King, and fear'd his God,
>   With upright heart and will.
> In social life sincere and just,
>   To vice of no kind given,
> So that his better part, we trust,
>   Hath made the port of Heaven.

Dubellay, an author of some repute, composed for LEON STOZZI, a seaman in the service of France, slain in Italy in 1554, an inscription somewhat as follows :—

I, the great Captain LEON STOZZI, I do not lie here in this urn, for so small an urn could not contain so great a man; earth holds me no longer, for a glory wider than the earth has raised me to heaven as a beautiful star for mariners, so that, as in the olden time the waters carried and sustained my ships, and trembled under me, even now it pleases me to become the God of the Sea. Go then, ye who follow me and are entrusted with my office, go boldly forth upon the waters; for there I have traced out for ye a safe and certain path.

In *South-hill* Church, *Bedfordshire*, is a plain monument to the memory of Admiral BYNG, who was shot at *Portsmouth* :—

> To the perpetual disgrace of public justice,
> The Honourable JOHN BYNG, Vice-Admiral of the Blue,
> fell a martyr to political persecution, *March* 14,
> in the year 1757;
> when bravery and loyalty were insufficient securities for
> the life and honour of a naval officer.

At *Carisbrook, Isle of Wight:*—

Here lieth the body of the Right Worthy WM. KEELING, Groom of the Chamber to our Sovereign Lord King James; General for the Hon. East India Adventures, whither he was thrice by them employed; and dying in this Isle at the age of 42, *An.* 1619, *Sept.* 19, hath this remembrance here fixed by his loving and sorrowful wife, Ann Keeling :—

> Fortie and two years in this vessel fraile
> On the rough seas of life did KEELING saile,
> A merchant fortunate, a captain bould,
> A courtier gracious, yet, alas! not old.

Such wealth, experience, honour, and high praise,
Few winne in twice so many years or days;
For what the world admired, he deem'd but drosse
For Christ,—without Christ all his gains but losse.
For Him and for His love, with merrie cheere,
To the Holy Land his last course he did steer:
Faith served for sails, the sacred word for yard;
Hope was his anchor, glorie his reward;
And thus with gales of grace, by happy venter,
Through straits of death, heav'n's harbour he did enter.

On a Sailor :—

Here goes honest BEN, to the sharks soon a prey,
Who lived like a sailor, good-natured and gay,
His rigging well fitted, his sides close and tight,
His bread-room well stow'd, and his mainmast aright.
Davy Jones, like a pirate built solely for plunder,
Thus hail'd the poor lad, in a voice harsh as thunder,
"Drop your peak, my tight fellow, your foresail throw back,
For already too long you've remain'd on that tack."
Ben heard the dread call, and without more ado,
His sail flatten'd in, and his bark she broach'd to.

At *Woodbridge, Suffolk.* On JOSEPH SPALDING, Master and Mariner, who departed this life *Sept.* 2, 1796, aged 55 :—

Embark'd in life's tempestuous sea, we steer
 Amidst threatening billows, rocks and shoals;
But Christ by faith dispels each wavering fear,
 And safe secures the anchor of our souls.

On a Military Officer, in a churchyard near *Oxford:*—

Billeted by Death,
 I quarter'd here lay slain;
And when the trumpet sounds,
 I'll rise and march again.

At *Yarmouth*:—

To the memory of ISAAC SMITH, who died *March* 24th, 1808, and SAMUEL BODGER, who died *April* 2nd, 1808, both of the *Cambridgeshire* Militia.

> The tyrant Death did early us arrest,
> And all the magazines of life possest:
> No more the blood its circling course did run,
> But in the veins like icicles it hung;
> No more the hearts, now void of quickening heat,
> The tuneful march of vital motion beat;
> Stiffness did into every sinew climb,
> And a short death crept cold through every limb.

At *Bury St. Edmunds*:—

WILLIAM MIDDLEDITCH,
Late Serjeant-Major of the Grenadier Guards,
Died *Nov.* 13, 1834, aged 53 years.

> A husband, father, comrade, friend sincere,
> A British soldier brave, lies buried here.
> In Spain and Flushing, and at Waterloo,
> He fought to guard our country from the foe;
> His comrades, Britons, who survive him, say,
> He acted nobly on that glorious day.

On an oval stone monument, against the south wall of St. Mary's Church, *Beverley, Yorkshire*, under two swords crossed:—

> Here two young Danish soldiers lie:
> The one in quarrel chanced to die;
> The other's head, by their own law,
> With sword was sever'd at one blow.

December 23rd, 1689.

At *Winchester.* To the memory of THOMAS FLETCHER:—

> Here sleeps in peace a Hampshire grenadier,
> Who caught his death by drinking cold small beer.
> Soldiers! take heed from his untimely fall,
> And when you're hot, drink strong, or none at all.

The stone, being decayed, was replaced by the officers of the garrison, A.D. 1781. This also failing, a stone with the following inscription was placed by the *North Hants* Militia, 1802:—

> An honest soldier never is forgot,
> Whether he die by musket or by pot.

At *Bremhill, Wiltshire.* On an old Soldier, aged 92:—

> A poor old soldier shall not lie unknown,
> Without a verse and this recording stone.
> 'Twas his, in youth, o'er distant lands to stray,
> Danger and death companions of his way.
> Here, in his native village, stealing age
> Closed the lone evening of his pilgrimage.
> Speak of the past—of names of high renown,
> Or brave commanders long to dust gone down,
> His look with instant animation glow'd,
> Tho' ninety winters on his head had snow'd.
> His country, while he lived, a boon supplied,
> And Faith her shield held o'er him when he died.

Epitaphium. On the Honble. Col. THOS. RAINSBROUGH, murdered in his bedchamber at *Doncaster*, by three Pontefract soldiers, Sunday, *October* 29, 1648:—

> Here lyes as much true valour as could dye,
> A sacrifice for England's Liberty,
> Great and good Rainsbrough (enough is said),
> Through Chomley's pride and cowardice betray'd.

The Epitaph, or Engravement, on the Tombstone :—

> He that made King, Lords, Commons, Judges shake,
>   Cities and Committees quake,
> He that sought nought but His dear countrie's good,
>   And seal'd their Right with His last blood,
> Rainsbrough, The Just, The Valiant, and True,
> Here bids the Noble Levellers Adieu.

In *Yarmouth* Churchyard :—

To the memory of GEORGE GRIFFITHS, of the *Shropshire* Militia, who died *Feb.* 26th, 1807, in consequence of a blow received in a quarrel with his comrade.

> Time flies away as nature on its wing.
> I in a battle died (not for my King.)
> Words with my brother soldier did take place,
> Which shameful is, and always brings disgrace.
> Think not the worse of him who do remain,
> For he as well as I might have been slain.

Upon the tomb of a General, named FRANCOIS DE MERCY, who died of wounds received in battle at *Nordlingen ;*—

> Stop, traveller, thou treadest upon a hero.

Again, in the famous battle of *Marathon*, in which the Greeks, under Miltiades, defeated the Persian army, and secured their independence, ÆSCHYLUS, a brave soldier, composed for himself the following :—

Here lies ÆSCHYLUS, son of Euphorion, born in *Attica.* He died in the fertile province of *Gela, Persia,* and the groves of *Marathon* will ever bear witness to his valour.

Chelsea Hospital. On a veteran :—

> Here lies WILLIAM HISELAND,
> A Veteran, if ever Soldier was,
> Who merited well a Pension,
> If long service be a merit,
> Having served upwards of the days of Man.
> Ancient, but not superannuated;
> Engaged in a Series of Wars,
> Civil as well as Foreign,
> Yet maimed or worn out by neither.
> His complexion was Fresh and Florid;
> His Health Hale and Hearty;
> His Memory Exact and Ready.
> In Stature,
> He exceeded the Military Size;
> In Strength,
> He surpassed the Prime of Youth;
> And
> What rendered his age still more Patriarchal,
> When above a Hundred Years old
> He took unto him a Wife!
> Read! fellow Soldiers, and reflect
> That there is a *Spiritual* Warfare,
> As well as a Warfare *Temporal.*
> Born the 1st *August,* 1620,
> Died the 17th of *February,* 1732,
> Aged One Hundred and Twelve.

In *Battersea* Church there is a handsome monument to Sir EDWARD WYNTER, a Captain in the East India Company's service in the reign of Charles II., which records that in *India*, where he had passed many years of his life, he was—

> A rare example, and unknown to most,
> Where wealth is gain'd, and conscience is not lost ;
> Nor less in martial honour was his name,
> Witness his actions of immortal fame.
> Alone, unharm'd, a tiger he opprest,
> And crush'd to death the monster of a beast.
> Thrice twenty mounted Moors he overthrew,
> Singly, on foot, some wounded, some he slew,
> Dispersed the rest,—what more could Samson do ?
> True to his friends, a terror to his foes,
> Here now in peace his honour'd bones repose.

Below, in bas-relief, he is represented struggling with the tiger, both the combatants appearing in the attitude of wrestlers. He is also depicted in the performance of the yet more wonderful achievement, the discomfiture of the "thrice twenty mounted Moors," who are all flying before him.

St. Giles' Church. A visitor to this place will not fail to remark a slab, and the following letters cut very deep into the marble :—

> Under this marble lie the bodies
> of the two most valiant Captains,
> Sir CHARLES LUCAS and Sir GEORGE LISLE, Knts.,
> Who, for their eminent Loyalty
> To their Sovereign,
> Were, on the 28th day of *August*, 1648,
> By command of Sir Thos. Fairfax,
> Then General of the Parliament Army,
> In cold blood barbarously murdered.

At *Little Stukely*, in *Huntingdonshire*. On the Rev. J. WATERHOUSE:—

>Sacred to the Memory of the
>Rev. JOSHUA WATERHOUSE, B.D.,
Nearly forty years fellow of Catherine Hall, Cambridge, Chaplain to his Majesty, Rector of this Parish, and of Coton, near Cambridge, who was inhumanly murdered *in this Parsonage House*, about ten o'clock on the morning of *July* 3rd, 1827. Aged 81.

>Beneath this tomb his mangled body's laid,
>Cut, stabb'd, and murder'd by Joshua Slade,
>His ghastly wounds a horrid sight to see,
>And hurl'd at once into eternity.

>What faults you've seen in him take care to shun,
>And look at home,—enough there's to be done;
>Death does not always warning give,
>Therefore be careful how you live.

At *Hackney:*—

>Sacred to the Memory of
>The Rev. DAVID GEORGE DAVIS,
>of this Parish,
>Who departed this life *Jan.* 10, 1812, aged 42 years,
>After a long affliction, which he bore
>With manly fortitude and steady faith.

>If dumb too long the drooping mate hath stay'd,
>And left her debt of sacred love unpaid;
>Blame not her silence, readers, but bemoan,
>And judge, oh judge my feelings by your own.
>To strew fresh laurels let the task be mine,
>A frequent pilgrim at thy sacred shrine;

> Mine, with true sighs thy absence to bemoan,
> And grave with faithful epitaph the stone:
> Live here on earth, preparing for the skies,
> Then at the last great day together rise;
> For God forbids the virtuous soul to die,
> Though we awhile may here united lie.

At *Lincoln* Cathedral, on the Rev. WILLIAM COLE, who died 1600:—

> Reader, behold the pious pattern here,
> Of true devotion and of holy fear:
> He sought God's glory, and the church's good,
> Idle idol worship firmly he withstood.
> Yet died in peace, whose body here doth lie,
> In expectation of eternity,
> And when the latter trump of heaven shall blow,
> COLE now *rak'd up in ashes* then shall *glow*.

We think that the survivors of the Rev. STEPHEN PENTON, a deceased clergyman, ought to have given him a different epitaph from the subjoined. Or, if he left it behind him, we cannot say that it evinces a very clear acquaintance with the Christianity which he professed to teach:—

Here lies what's left of STEPHEN PENTON, rector, who, being dead, yet speaketh once for all. My beloved Parishioners, since any of you may be the next, let every one prepare to be so. To prepare for death devoutly, receive the Sacrament often, and make your will while you are in good health, that you may have leisure to die wisely. And if you hope to die comfortably, you must resolve to live righteously. God send us all a happy meeting.

From *Godalming* Churchyard, *Surrey*. On the Rev. O. MANNING, the county historian :—

> This stone
> Is erected as a token of that respect and esteem
> so justly due to the memory of the distinguishedly
> worthy man whose remains are deposited here,
> The Rev. OWEN MANNING,
> B.D., Canon of Lincoln, Rector of Peperhárrow,
> Vicar of this Parish upwards of 37 years ;
> Also F.R.S. and F.S.A.
> He departed this life the 9th of *September*, 1801,
> in the 81st year of his age.
> All his professional duties were discharged with
> great punctuality and efficacy, and his
> Deportment through life was an amiable example
> of that rectitude of conduct and universal benevolence
> so perfectly consistent with those evangelical truths
> which he had so long, so rationally, and so forcibly
> impressed upon his auditors !

Ancient Inscription. In the reign of Mary, 1556, the reverend and pious Dr. ROWLAND TAYLOR was burnt alive on a common within a mile of the town of *Hadleigh*, in *Suffolk*, for his undaunted defence of the Protestant faith, and on this spot where he suffered martyrdom was found a stone with the following inscription :—

> D. Taylor in def-
> ending that was gode,
> At this plase
> Left his blod.

This stone was railed round in the year 1730, and is

still, or was a few years since, in a tolerably good state of preservation.

In *Chigwell* Church, *Essex*, is the statue of Archbishop HARSNETT in brass, standing on a pedestal, dressed in his episcopalia, with his mitre and crosier; he had been vicar of this place.

On J. COTTON, a *New England* preacher, died 1652:—

He was in truth a living Bible endowed with breath, where the two Covenants were inscribed; the Gospel and the Law had each their column in his heart. His head was the index of the Holy Volume; his name (COTTON) the title, and his life a commentary upon the text. Oh, what a worthy and precious monument when he shall reappear in a new edition, without errata; he will then be rebound for Eternity!

On — COLNETT, Curate of *Waltham* Abbey for 14 years:—

>   Shall pride a heap of sculptured marble raise,
>   Some worthless unmourn'd titled fool to praise,
>   And shall we not by one poor gravestone know
>   Where pious worthy Colnett sleeps below?

Another, in honour of ALPHONSE-LOUIS DU PLESSIS, Cardinal of Lyons, and brother of Cardinal Richelieu:—

>   A pauper born, and vow'd e'en so I die,
>   And amidst paupers I would wish to lie.

On an Abbot, who died in 1126:—

He was a lover of peace, I pray now that he may rest in peace.

Lincoln Cathedral. On MICHAEL HONEYWOOD, D.D.:—

Here lieth the Body of
MICHAEL HONEYWOOD, D.D.,
Dean of *Lincoln*, who died *Sept.* 7, 1681, aged 85.
He was Grandchild, and one of the 367 persons
That Mary,* the Wife of Robert Honeywood, Esq.,
Did see before she died lawfully descended from her;
That is,
Sixteen of her own body,
One hundred and fourteen Grandchildren,
Two hundred and twenty-eight of the third generation,
And nine of the fourth.

On JOHN ILGER, Prior of *St. Barbara, Normandy:*—

Aspiring after peace.

On the Rev. Mr. BEIGHTON, who had been vicar of *Egham* forty-five years:—

Near half an age, with every good man's praise,
Among his flock the Shepherd pass'd his days:
The friend, the comfort of the sick and poor;
Want never knock'd unheeded at his door;
Oft, when his duty call'd, disease and pain
Strove to confine him, but they strove in vain.
All moan his death, his virtues long they tried,
They knew not how they loved him till he died.
Peculiar blessings did his life attend,
He had no foe, and Camden was his friend.

---

* The Lady Mary Honeywood, mentioned above, died at Markshall, in Essex, in 1620, aged 92 years, and in the 44th year of her widowhood.

East Barnet, Hertfordshire. On ROBERT TAYLOR :—

    Here lies the Body of
     ROBERT TAYLOR,
Late Rector of *East Barnet*, and Prebendary of
      Lincoln,
  Whose solid and useful Learning,
   Judicious and steady Zeal
For the Doctrine and Discipline of the Church of
      England,
   Had rendered him valuable
   To all sincere Lovers thereof.
     After he had,
 For above the Space of Forty-two Years,
   Recommended true Piety,
   By his Preaching and Example,
   He left, by his last Will,
   That excellent Book, intituled
   The Whole Duty of Man,
   To every Family in his Parish,
     As an Instance
Of his dying Care and Concern for their Souls.
  Obiit. Feb. 18, 1718. *Ætat* 72.

In the village of *Kirkmichael,* was the home scene of BISHOP WILSON'S active benevolence, for more than half a century; he was loved and esteemed for his goodness, by all ranks and degrees of men. The end of this good man was easy and tranquil, it was like his life devoted to prayer and praise, till he fell asleep to wake in Heaven. He was attended to the grave by the whole population of the *Isle of Man,* without a single exception, unless of those who by age or sickness were incapacitated. He was interred in *Kirkmichael* Churchyard, at the east end, near the chancel, and over his grave a square tombstone is placed, surrounded by iron rails, on which is the following inscription :—

On the sides :

Sleeping in Jesus, here lieth the body of THOMAS WILSON, D.D., Lord Bishop of this isle, who died *March* 5, 1755, aged 93, and in the 58th year of his consecration.

At the ends :

This monument was erected by his Son, Thomas Wilson, a native of this parish, who in obedience to the express commands of his father, declines giving him the character he justly deserved.

Let this island speak the rest.

St. Clement's Danes, Strand. On JOSEPH MILLER, (by S. Duck) :—

>Here lie the remains of
>Honest JOE MILLER,
>Who was
>A tender Husband,
>A sincere friend,
>A facetious Companion,
>And an excellent Comedian.
>He departed this life the 15th day of August, 1738,
>Aged 54 years.

If Humour, Wit, and Honesty could save
The Humorous, Witty, Honest, from the grave,
The Grave had not so soon this tenant found,
Whom Honesty, and Wit, and Humour crown'd ;
Or could Esteem and Love preserve our Breath,
And guard us longer from the stroke of Death,

> The stroke of Death on him had later fell,
> Whom all mankind esteem'd and loved so well.

Clifton, Gloucestershire. On JOHN HIPPISLEY, Comedian :—

> When the Stage heard that Death had struck her JOHN,
> Gay *Comedy* her Sables first put on ;
> *Laughter* lamented that her Fav'rite died,
> And *Mirth* herself ('tis strange) lay down and cry'd.
> *Wit* droop'd his head, e'en *Humour* seem'd to mourn,
> And solemnly sat pensive o'er his urn.

On SAMUEL FOOTE :—

> FOOTE from this earthly stage, alas! is hurl'd;
> Death took him off who took off all the world.

In *Chiswick* Churchyard is Garrick's Epitaph on WILLIAM HOGARTH, (died Oct. 29, 1764, aged 67 years,) as follows :—

> Farewell, great painter of mankind,
>   Who reach'd the noblest point of art,
> Whose pictured morals charm the mind,
>   And thro' the eye correct the heart.
>
> If genius fire thee, reader, stay;
>   If nature touch thee, drop a tear;
> If neither move thee, turn away,
>   For HOGARTH'S honour'd dust lies here.
>
> No marble pomp, or monumental praise,
> My tomb, this dial—epitaph, these lays ;
> Pride and low mouldering clay but ill agree;
> Death levels me to beggars—Kings to me.
>
> Alive, instruction was my work each day;
> Dead, I persist instruction to convey:
> Here, reader, mark, perhaps now in thy prime,
> The stealthy steps of *never-standing Time:*
> Thou'lt be what I am—catch the present hour,
> Employ that well, for that's within thy power.

The following *Epitaph* is supposed to have been written by *Shakspeare*, who died 23rd *April*, 1616, the anniversary of his birth, having exactly completed his 52nd year. He was buried on the north side of the chancel in the church at *Stratford-upon-Avon* :—

> Good Friend for Iesus Sake forbare
> To diGG T—E Dust EncloAsed HERe.
> Blese be T—E Man $\frac{T}{Y}$ spares T—Es Stones
> And curst be He $\frac{T}{Y}$ moves my Bones.

Literal translation :—

> Good friend, for Jesus' sake forbear
> To dig the dust enclosed here;
> Blest be the man who spares these stones,
> And curst be he that moves my bones!

The following lines were written by Ben Jonson, and are under the effigy of his companion and friend SHAKSPEARE :—

> The figure that thou here seest put,
> It was for gentle SHAKSPEARE cut,
> Wherein the graver had a strife
> With Nature to outdo the life;
> O, could he but have drawne his wit
> As well in brass as he has hit
> His face, the print would then surpass
> All that was ever writ in brass;
> But since he cannot, reader looke,
> Not on his picture, but his booke!

SHAKSPEARE'S monument at *Stratford-upon-Avon* :—

> Great *Homer's* birth sev'n rival cities claim,
> Too mighty such monopoly of Fame,

> Yet not to birth alone did Homer owe
> His wondrous worth : what *Egypt* could bestow,
> With all the schools of *Greece* and *Asia* join'd,
> Enlarged the immense expansion of his mind,
> Nor yet unrivall'd the *Mæonian* strain.
> The *British Eagle* and the *Mantuan Swan*
> Tower-equal heights. But happier *Stratford*, thou
> With uncontested laurels deck thy brow:
> Thy *Bard* was thine UNSCHOOLED, and from thee brought
> More than all *Egypt, Greece*, or *Asia* taught ;
> Not Homer's self such matchless honours won,
> The *Greek* has *Rivals*, but thy *Shakspeare* none!

The following is a record of the wit, piety, and humanity of Mrs. SUSANNAH HALL, daughter of SHAKSPEARE, died July, 1649, aged 66, also buried in *Stratford* Church. The lines do not now appear on the stone, but they have been preserved by Dugdale, the Antiquarian :—

> Witty above her sexe, but that's not all,
> Wise to Salvation was good Mistress HALL ;
> Something of Shakspeare was in that, but this
> Wholly of Him with whom she's now in bliss.
> Then, passenger, hast ne'er a teare
> To weep with her that wept with all
> That wept, yet she herselfe to chere
> Them up with comfort's cordiall.
> Her love shall live, her mercy spread,
> When thou hast ne'er a tear to shed!

In a small MS. volume of Poems, by Herrick and others, in the handwriting of Charles I., preserved in the Bodleian library, is an *Epitaph ascribed to Shakspeare* :—

> When God was pleased, the world unwilling yet,
> Elias James to nature pay'd his debt,

And here reposeth ; as he lived, he dyde,
The saying in him strongly verified.
Such life, such death, then the known truth to tell,
He lived a godly life, and dyde as well.
                              WM. SHAKSPEARE.

Sir William Dugdale, in his Visitation Book, describes a monument in Tongue Church, *Salop*, erected in memory of SIR THOMAS STANLEY, who died about the year 1600.

The following verses were made by William Shakspeare, the late famous tragedian :—

Aske who lyes here, but do not weepe ;
He is not dead, he doth but sleep !
This stony register is for his bones,
His fame is more perpetual than these stones.
And his own goodness, with himself being gone,
Shall live, when earthly monument is none.

Not monumental stone preserves our fame,
Nor sky-aspiring pyramids our name:
The memory of him for whom this stands,
Shall outlive marble, and defacers' hands !
When *all* to *Time's* consumption shall be given,
Stanley, for whom this *stands*, shall *stand* in heaven.

In St. Mary Magdalen Church, *Richmond, Surrey*, is this inscription on a brass tablet :—

In the earth below this tablet are the remains of JAMES THOMSON, author of the beautiful poems entitled " The Seasons," " The Castle of Indolence," etc., who died at *Richmond*, the 27th of August, and was buried here on the 29th, old stile, 1748. The Earl of Buchan, unwilling that so good a man and sweet a poet should be without a memorial, has denoted the place of his interment for the satisfaction of his admirers, in the year of our Lord 1792.

Underneath is a quotation from the " Winter " :—

> Father of Light and Life ! Thou Good Supreme !
> O teach me what is good ! Teach me *Thyself!*
> Save me from following vanity and vice,
> From every low pursuit ! and feed my soul
> With knowledge, conscious peace, and virtue pure ;
> Sacred, substantial, never-fading bliss.

Westminster Abbey. On SAMUEL BUTLER˙:—

> Sacred to the Memory of
> SAMUEL BUTLER,
> Who was born
> At *Strensham,* in *Worcestershire,* 1612,
> And died in *London,* 1680.
> Of Uncommon Wit, Learning, and Probity,
> As admirable for the products of his Genius,
> As Unhappy in the Rewards of them.
> His Satire
> Exposing the Hypocrisy and Wickedness of the Rebels,
> Is such an inimitable Piece,
> That as he was the First,
> He may be said to be also the Last Writer,
> In his peculiar manner,
> That he,
> Who when living wanted almost everything,
> Might not after Death
> Any longer want so much as a tomb.
> John Barber,
> Citizen of *London,* erect. this Monument, 1721.

On BUTLER'S monument in *Westminster* Abbey, by S. Westley :—

> Whilst Butler, needy wretch ! was yet alive,
> No gen'rous patron would a dinner give.
> See him, when starved to death, and turn'd to dust,
> Presented with a monumental bust.
> The Poet's fate is here in emblem shown ;
> He ask'd for bread, and he received a stone.

Epitaph on JOHN GAY, by himself :—

> Life is a jest, and all things show it ;
> I thought so once, but now I know it.

On PAUL WHITEHEAD, Poet and Satirist :—

> Here lies a man misfortune could not bend ;
> Praised as a poet, honour'd as a friend :
> Tho' his youth kindled with the love of fame,
> Within his bosom glow'd a brighter flame.
> Where'er his friends with sharp affliction bled,
> And from the wounded deer the herd was fled,
> Whitehead stood forth—the healing balm applied,
> Nor quitted their distresses—till he died.

The late WALTER SAVAGE LANDOR left the subjoined lines as his own Epitaph :—

> I strove with none, for none were worth my strife ;
> Nature I loved, and after Nature, Art.
> I warm'd both hands before the fire of life ;
> It sinks, and I am ready to depart.

On SAMUEL TAYLOR COLERIDGE, Poet, who died 25th *July*, 1834, written by himself :—

> Stop, Christian passer-by ; stop, child of God !
> And read with gentle breast. Beneath this sod

A poet lies, or that which once seem'd he ;—
Oh, lift a thought in prayer for S. T. C. !
That he who many a year with toil of breath,
Found death in life, may here find life in death !
Mercy for praise,—to be forgiven, for fame,
He asked, and hoped through Christ—Do thou the same.

On JAMES QUIN, in *Bath* Cathedral, by D. Garrick :—

That tongue, which set the table in a roar,
And charm'd the public ear, is heard no more ;
Closed are those eyes, the harbingers of wit,
Which spoke, before the tongue, what Shakspeare writ ;
Cold are those hands, which, living, were stretch'd forth,
At friendship's call, to succour modest worth.
Here is James Quin ! Deign, reader to be taught,
Whate'er thy strength of body, force of thought,
In Nature's happiest mould however cast,
"To this complexion thou must come at last."

Epitaph, written by Herrick, upon BEN JONSON :—

Here lies Jonson with the rest
Of the poets, but the best,
Reader, wouldst thou more have known ?
Ask his story, not this stone ;
That will speak what this can't tell
Of his glory. So farewell.

Pennycrick, Mid-Lothian. Here is an obelisk raised to the memory of ALLAN RAMSAY, the Poet.

St. Margaret's, *Westminster.* On JOSEPH SKELTON, the merry Poet-Laureate to Henry VII. and VIII., died 21 *June,* 1529 :—

Come, *Alecto,* and lend me thy Torch
To find a Church-yard in a Church-porch.
Povertie and Poetrie this Tomb doth inclose,
Therefore, Gentlemen, be merry in Prose.

Translation of the Epitaph on VIRGIL and TIBULLUS, by Lord Byron :—

> He, who sublime in epic numbers roll'd,
> And he who struck the softer lyre of love,
> By Death's unequal hand alike controll'd,
> Fit comrades in Elysian regions move!

On OLIVER GOLDSMITH, by D. Garrick :—

> Here lies poet Goldsmith, for shortness called Noll,
> Who wrote like an angel, but talked like poor Poll.

SCARRON, a comic poet of considerable talent, who all his life suffered from a complication of diseases, wrote his own epitaph in a spirit which, under affected levity, strives to conceal the deepest melancholy :—

> Pity, not envy, be the lot
> Of him who lieth here! I wot
> A thousand deaths he long endured,
> Until by Death his ills were cured.
> Stranger, pass on, and make no riot—
> Take care he slumbers on in quiet,
> Nor break the only sleep ('tis true!)
> Unhappy SCARRON ever knew.

In *Halesowen* Churchyard, *Shropshire*, a small stone pillar is erected to the memory of the Poet WILLIAM SHENSTONE, with the following inscription :—

> Whoe'er thou art, with rev'rence tread
> These sacred mansions of the dead;
> Not that the monumental bust
> Or sumptuous tomb here guards the dust
> Of rich or great, (let wealth, rank, birth,
> Sleep undistinguish'd in the earth.)
> This simple urn records a name
> That shines with most exalted fame.

Reader! if genius, taste refined,
A native elegance of mind;
If virtue, science, manly sense;
If wit that never gave offence;
The clearest head, the tenderest heart,
In thy esteem e'er claim'd a part,
Ah, smite thy breast, and drop a tear,
For know that SHENSTONE'S dust lies here.

Inscription on the tomb of BLOOMFIELD, in *Campton* Churchyard, *Bedfordshire* :—

Here lie
The Remains of
ROBERT BLOOMFIELD.
He was born at Honington,
in Suffolk,
December III., MDCCLXVI,
And died at Shefford,
August XIX., MDCCCXXIII.
Let his wild native woodnotes tell the rest.

This stone was erected at the expense of Henry Kaye Bonney, D.D., late Archdeacon of Bedford, who also composed the inscription.

On the Poet BLOOMFIELD :—

Humble he enter'd in the world of strife;
Humble he lived, and humble was he bred;
Poverty awaited on his steps through life,
And in Adversity's sad page he deeply read.

No stately monument for him attracts the eye,
No flattering epitaphs pronounce his fame;
His mould'ring form beneath the sod doth lie;
His works alone must tell his humble name.

III.

𝔚itty and 𝔊rotesque.

The imperious necessity of rhyme is well illustrated in the following touching epitaph :—

>Under this stone, agèd threescore and ten,
>Lie the remains of WILLIAM WOOD-HEN.

N.B.—For -HEN read -COCK. Cock wouldn't come in rhyme.

Epitaph :—

>Here lies JOHN BUNN,
>Who was kill'd by a gun.
>His name wasn't BUNN, but his real name was WOOD,
>But WOOD wouldn't rhyme with gun, so I thought BUNN would.

Another :—

>This little hero that lies here
>Was conquer'd by the diarrheer.

Another :—

>Here lies the wife of SIMON STOKES,
>Who lived and died—like other folks.

In *St. Giles's* Churchyard, *Northampton* :—

Here lies a most dutiful daughter, honest and just,
Awaiting the resurrection, in hopes to be one of the first.

On a lady whose name was STONE :—

Curious enough, we all must say,
That what was *Stone* should now be clay,
More curious still, to own we must,
That what was *Stone* will soon be dust.

In a churchyard near *Newmarket* lie buried the two wives of Tom Sexton, on the tombstone of one is the following :—

Here lies the body of SARAH SEXTON,
She was a wife that never vexed one;
I can't say so much for the one at the next stone.

On a miser named MORE :—

Iron was his chest,
Iron was his door,
His hand was iron,
And his heart was *more*.

On a miser :—

You'd have me say, Here lies T. U.,
But I do not believe it;
For after death there's something due,
And he's gone to receive it,

On a miser :—

Here lies one who for med'cines would not give
A little gold, and so his life he lost;
I fancy now he'd wish again to live,
Could he but guess how much his funeral cost.

On BANCROFT, Archbishop of Canterbury, a very covetous man :—

> Here lies his grace in cold clay clad,
> Who died for want of what he had.

On a miser :—

> Reader, beware immoderate love of pelf ;
> Here lies the worst of thieves—who robb'd himself.

Another :—

Here lies Old Father Gripe, who never cried, " Iam satis ;"
'Twould wake him did he know you read his tombstone gratis.

On the monument of a miser :—

> The wretched man who moulders here
> Cared not for soul or body lost,
> But only wept when death drew near,
> To think how much his tomb would cost.

Epitaphs are frequently fostered on some celebrated man ; this we find to be Shakspeare's case. The story of the epitaph of a rich usurer named COMBS is variously told. One is supposed to be made extempore at a tavern in Stratford :—

> Ten in the hundred the devil allowes,
> But COMBS will have twelve he sweares and vowes,
> If any aske who lies in this tombe,
> "Hoh," quoth the devil, "'tis my JOHN-O-COMBE."

In *another version* the wit is certainly heightened. Mr. JOHN COMBE has amassed considerable wealth. He was Shakspeare's intimate friend. In the gaiety of conversation he told the poet that he fancied he intended to furnish his epitaph, and since whatever might be said of him after he was dead must be unknown to him, he requested it might be written forthwith. The bard immediately gave him the following verse :—

>Ten in the hundred lies here engraved,
>'Tis a hundred to ten his soul is not saved:
>If any man ask who lies in this tomb,
>"Oh! oh!" quoth the devil, "'tis my JOHN-O-COMBE."

Again we find Peck, in his memoirs of Milton (4to. 1740) has introduced *another epitaph*, which he attributes, though it does not appear on what authority, to Shakspeare. It is on a TOM-O-COMBE, otherwise " *Thin beard,*" brother to the above-named John :—

>Thin in beard, and thick in purse,
>Never man beloved worse,
>He went to the grave with many a curse.
>The devil and he had both one nurse.

In the choir of *Wymondham* Church, *Norfolk*, a gentleman was interred named " NONE," who not having been, according to expectation, liberal to the convent, one of the monks wrote a pointed epitaph in Latin to his memory, which, translated by an ancient bard, read thus :—

>Here lyeth *None*, who worse than *none* was thought,
>For being none, of *none* to Christ gave nought.

At *Elsham, Northamptonshire* :—

>My name it was NATHANIEL FREER,
>I lived and laugh'd, but now I'm here.
>Such as I am, such you must be ;
>Then make your game, and follow me.

On a writer of long epitaphs :—

>Friend, in your epitaphs I'm grieved
>   So very much is said.
>One half will never be believed,
>   The other never read.

In *Westminster* Abbey. On SAMUEL FOOTE, the Comedian :—

> Here lies one *Foote*, whose death may thousands save,
> For death has now one *foot* within the grave.

The following epitaph is copied *verbatim* from a headstone in a graveyard near *Philadelphia* :—

In memory of HENRY WANG, son of his Father and Mother, John and Maria Wang. Died *Dec.* 31st, 1829, aged 1-2 hour. The first deposit of this yard.

> A short-lived joy
> Was our little boy.
> He has gone on high,
> So don't you cry.

At *Pewsey*, in *Bedfordshire* :—

> Here lies the body of
> Lady O'LOONEY,
> Great-niece of Burke, commonly
> called the Sublime.
> She was
> Bland, passionate, and deeply religious;
> Also she painted in water colours,
> And sent several pictures to the Exhibition.
> She was first cousin to Lady Jones,
> And of such is the kingdom of heaven.

On GROSE, the Antiquary :—

> Here lies FRANCIS GROSE.
> On Thursday, *May* 12, 1791,
> Death put an end to
> His *views* and *prospects*.

Epitaph on a hermit :—

> For years upon a mountain's brow,
> A hermit lived, the Lord knows how;
> A robe of sackcloth he did bear,
> And got his food, the Lord knows where.
> Hardships and penance were his lot;
> He often pray'd, the Lord knows what.
> At length this holy man did die;
> He left this world, the Lord knows why.
> He's buried in this gloomy den,
> And he shall rise, the Lord knows when.

At *Cherening-le-Clay, Dorsetshire*. After recording the death of his beloved wife, ANN HUGHES, the afflicted husband breaks forth in this pious strain :—

> Who far below this tomb doth rest,
> Has join'd the army of the blest.
> The Lord has ta'en her to the sky,
> The saints rejoice, and so do I.

Another curious specimen in the *Old Grey Friars, Edinburgh* :—

> Here snug in grave my wife doth lie,
> Now she's at rest, and so am I.

In *Lymington* Churchyard, *Hampshire* :—

> Live well, die never;
> Die well, live for ever.

On FREDERICK, Prince of Wales, Father of George III. :—

> Here lies PRINCE FRED,
> Gone down among the dead;
> Had it been his father,
> We had much rather;

> Had it been his mother,
> Better than any other;
> Had it been his sister,
> We ne'er should have miss'd her;
> Had it been the whole generation,
> Ten times better for the nation;
> But since it is only Fred,
> There's no more to be said.

A somewhat similar one in the Churchyard of *St. Hilary, Cornwall* :—

> Here lies NED,
> I'm glad he's dead;
> If there must be another,
> I wish 'twere his brother,
> And for the good of the nation
> His whole generation.

The following is a beautiful instance of conjugal affection :—

> Here lies my dear wife, a sad slattern and shrew;
> If I said I regretted her, I should lie too.

Another :—

> When you look on my grave,
> And behold how they wave,
> The cypress, the yew, and the willow,
> You think 'tis the breeze,
> That gives motion to these—
> 'Tis the laughter that's shaking my pillow.
> I must laugh when I see,
> A poor insect like thee
> Dare to pity the fate thou must own,
> Let a few moments slide,
> We shall lie side by side,
> And crumble to dust bone for bone.
> Go, weep thine own doom,
> Thou wert born for the tomb —

> Thou hast lived, like myself, but to die.
> Whilst thou pity'st my lot,
> Secure fool, thou'st forgot
> Thou art no more immortal than I.

Sometimes a salutary truth is rendered almost ridiculous by the ingenuity of the lapidary. From *Cunwallow*, near *Helstone, Cornwall*:—

Shall	wee	all	die?
Wee	shall	die	all.
All	die	shall	we?
Die	all	we	shall.

West Grinstead Churchyard, *Sussex*:—

> Vast, strong was I, but yet did die,
> And in my grave asleep I lie.
> My grave is stoned round about,
> Yet I hope the Lord will find me out.

Hadleigh Church, *Suffolk*:—

> The charnel mounted on this w \
> Sets to be seen in funer \
> A matron playn domestic \
> In housewifery a princip \
> In care and payns continu \
> Not slow, nor gay, nor prodig   all. \
> Yet neighbourly and hospit \
> Her children seven yet living \
> Her sixty-seventh year hence did c \
> To rest her body natur \
> In hope to rise spiritu

ELLEN, wife of ROBERT RESON, Alderman of this town. Shee deceased *January* 8th, 1630, and is interred below hereby.

On a solicitor, in *Rineton* Churchyard, *Norfolk*:—

> God works a wonder now and then,
> He, though a lawyer, was an honest man.

In *St. Michael's* Churchyard, *Coventry*. On Mrs. WOODIER :—

> She was——
> But words are wanting
>   To say what.
> Look what a wife *should* be,
> And *she was that*.

The Greeks occasionally indulged in satiric inscriptions. Simonides composed an epitaph for TIMOCREON, a wrestler and satirical rhymester :—

Here lies TIMOCREON the Rhodian, who spent his days in eating, drinking, and slandering everybody !

The line hereunder was written upon one TRIVULCIUS, a man of restless and adventurous disposition :—

> Here rests he who never rested !

Another :—

> I was well. I took physic.
> I am here !

In *St. Peter's* Churchyard, *Isle of Thanet* :—

> Against his will
> Here lies GEORGE HILL,
> Who from a cliff
> Fell down quite stiff.
> When it happen'd is not known,
> Therefore not mention'd on this stone.

In *St. James's* Church, *Piccadilly, London*. On TOM D'URFEY :—

> Here lies the Lyric, who, with tale and song,
> Did life to threescore years and ten prolong;
> His tale was pleasant, and his song was sweet,
> His heart was cheerful, but his thirst was great.
> Grieve, reader, grieve that he too soon grew old—
> His song is ended, and his tale is told.

In the Churchyard of *St. Mary, Islington* :—

    Censure not rashly, though nature's apt to halt,
    No woman's born that dies without a fault.

On JOHN HILL, at *Manchester* :—

        Here lies JOHN HILL,
        A man of skill,
    His age was five times ten;
        He ne'er did good,
        Nor ever would,
    Had he lived as long again.

On Miss ARABELLA YOUNG, a loquacious lady :—

    Here rests, in silent clay,
      Miss ARABELLA YOUNG,
    Who on the 21st of May,
      Began to hold her tongue.

On a workhouse pauper :—

        THORP'S
        Corpse.

On an infant :—

        She never told her love.

On two lovers :—

    The first deceased; he for a little tried
    To live without her—liked it not—then died

On a wife :—

    She once was mine;
          And now
    To thee, O Lord, I her resign;
    And am your obedient humble servant,
        ROBERT KEMP.

From a churchyard in *Hereford* :—

> *Woman.*
> Grieve not for me, my husband dear,
> I am not dead, but sleeping, here;
> With patience wait—prepare to die—
> And in short time you'll come to I.
>
> *Man.*
> I am not grieved, my dearest life,
> Sleep on—I've got another wife;
> Therefore, I cannot come to thee,
> For I must go and live with she.

In *Halstead* Churchyard, *Essex*, on an iron tomb :—

> Silence.

On a talkative old maid (1750) :—

> Beneath this silent stone is laid
> A noisy, antiquated maid,
> Who from her cradle talk'd till death,
> And ne'er before was out of breath.

In *Matharn* Churchyard, *Monmouthshire*. On JOHN LEE :—

> Here lies JOHN LEE, that good old man;
> We ne'er will see him more.
> He used to wear an old brown coat,
> All button'd down before.

In *Dawlish* Churchyard, *Devonshire*, and at *Kingsbridge*. On a man who was too poor to be buried with his relations in the church :—

> Here I lie at ye church door,
> Here I lie, because I'se poor.
> Ye furder you go, ye more you pay,
> Here I lie as warm as they.

Same place:—

> Who lies here? who do you think?
> Old JOHN JACKSON. *Make* him drink!
> Make a dead man drink! for why?
> When he was alive, he was always dry.

In *Old St. Pancras, Middlesex*:—

> I am here, I am there, do you know where?
> When I was alive, 'twas that made me stare.

On Mr. BOX:—

> Here lies one *Box* within another,
> The one of wood was very good,
> We cannot say so much for t'other.

In *Cheltenham* Churchyard:—

Here lies the body of MOLLY DICKIE, the Wife of HALL DICKIE, tailor.

> Two great physicians first
> My loving husband tried,
> To cure my pain—
> In vain,
> At last he got a third,
> And then I died.

On Sir THOMAS WOODCOCK, Lord Mayor of *London*, 1405:—

> Hic jacet, TOM SHORTHOSE,
> Sine tomb, sine sheets, sine riches;
> Ni vixit sine gown,
> Sine cloak, sine shirt, sine breeches.

From the Greek. (Cowper.) On an old bachelor:—

> At threescore winters' end I died,
>   A cheerless being, sole and sad;
> The nuptial knot I never tied,
>   And wish my father never had.

On an Irish chairman:—

> Weep, Irish lads, all true and fair men;
> Here rests the leader of the chairmen.
> Reader, rejoice that here lies Pat,
> For was he up he'd lay you flat.
> In *fame*, you'll never see his brother,
> It reach'd from one *pole* to the other;
> And would you know him when an angel fair,
> You've nothing more to do than call, Chair! chair!

On a stump orator:—

> Here lies a witless dog, who had the wit
> To make men think he had no lack of it.
> As his own tongue, his life was always loose;
> But his loose tongue his looseness did excuse.
> He nothing knew, yet men believed he taught;
> His words were many, but their value nought.
> The fools who listen'd thought his notes were gold;
> And, to speak truth, for that they oft were sold.
> He was as coarse a specimen of clay
> As ever clogged a hole, or stopp'd the way.
> His name was *Mudd*, his ways were in the slime,
> While life's oil'd wheels ran o'er the shores of time.
> But when death's drought came on, as come it must,
> He dried into a little heap of dust.

On the Earl of KILDARE, by Dean Swift:—

> Who *kill'd Kildare?* Who *dared Kildare to kill?*
> Death *kill'd Kildare*—who *dare kill* whom he will.

In a *Wiltshire* Churchyard :—

> Beneath this steane lies our deare child, who's gone from we,
> For evermore unto Eternity,
> Where us do hope, that we shall go to he,
> But him can ne'er go back to we.

Epitaph on the death of STEPHEN REMNANT, Esq., of *Woolwich* :—

> Here's a *remnant* of life, and a *remnant* of death,
> Taken off both at once in a *remnant* of breath,
> To mortality this gives a happy release,
> For what was the *remnant* proves now the *whole piece*.

Broom Churchyard, *Bedfordshire*. The following is a family epitaph :—

> God be praised!
> Here is Mr. DUDLEY, Senior,
> And JANE his wife also,
> Who while living was his superior,
> But see what death can do;
> Two of his sons also lie here,
> One WALTER, t'other JOE,
> They all of them went in the year
> 1510 *below*.

Tiverton Church, *Devonshire*. On the Earl of DEVONSHIRE, and his wife :—

> Ho! ho! who lies here?
> 'Tis I, the Earl of Devonshire,
> With Kate, my wife, to me full dear;
> We lived together fifty-five year.
> That we spent we had,
> That we left we lost,
> That we gave we have.

San Salvador, Oviedo. At the entrance of the Church at this place, is a most remarkable tomb, erected by a prince named Silo, with the following curious inscription, which may be read 270 different ways, beginning with the capital (S) in the centre:—

Silo Princeps Fecit.

On the tomb are likewise inscribed these letters:—

H. E. S. S. S. S. T. L.

The meaning of which is *Hic est Silo situs, sit sibi terra levis.* In English, Here Silo lies buried; may the earth be light upon him.

```
T I C E F S P E C N C E P S F E C I T
I C E F S P E C N I N C E P S F E C I
C E F S P E C N I R I N C E P S F E C
E F S P E C N I R P R I N C E P S F E
F S P E C N I R P O P R I N C E P S F
S P E C N I R P O L O P R I N C E P S
P E C N I R P O L I L O P R I N C E P
E C N I R P O L I S I L O P R I N C E
P E C N I R P O L I L O P R I N C E P
S P E C N I R P O L O P R I N C E P S
F S P E C N I R P O P R I N C E P S F
E F S P E C N I R P R I N C E P S F E
C E F S P E C N I R I N C E P S F E C
I C E F S P E C N I N C E P S F E C I
T I C E F S P E C N C E P S F E C I T
```

At *Fosbrooke,* in *Northumberland:*—

> Here lieth MATTHEW HOLLINGSHEAD,
> Who died from cold caught in his head.
> It brought on fever and rheumatiz,
> Which ended me—for here I is.

Epitaph said to have been written in pencil on a tombstone, by Lord Byron, when a boy:—

>Beneath these *green trees*, rising to the skies,
>The planter of them, Isaac *Greentree* lies;
>A time shall come when these *green trees* shall fall,
>And Isaac *Greentree* rise above them all.

In a *Sussex* Churchyard:—

RICHARD BASSET, the old clerk of this parish, who had continued the office of clerk and sexton for the space of forty-three years, whose melody was warbled forth as if he had been thumped on the back with a stone, was buried on the 20th *September*, 1866.

Epitaph, from the French:—

>Careless and thoughtless all my life,
>Stranger to every source of strife;
>And deeming each grave sage a fool,
>The Law of Nature was my rule,
>By which I learnt to duly measure
>My portion of desire and pleasure.
>'Tis strange that here I lie, you see;
>   For Death must have indulged a whim,
>At any time t' have thought of me,
>   Who never once did think of him.

In *Guilsfield* Churchyard. On DAVID WILLIAMS 1769:—

>Under this yew-tree,
>Buried would he be,
>Because his father—he
>Planted this yew-tree.

The following epitaph may be seen in the Cemetery of *Montmartre*:—

Poor CHARLES!
His innocent pleasure was to row on the water.
Alas!
He was the victim of this fatal desire,
Which conducted him to the tomb.
Reader! Consider that the water in which he was drowned
Is the amassed tears of his relatives and friends.

At *St. Ives, Cornwall*, is a monument on the family of SISE, which insipidly informs us:—

Neere to this bed sixe *Sises* late were laid,
Four hopefull sons, ye grandsire, and a maid.

On Sir JOHN GUISE:—

Here lies Sir JOHN GUISE:
No one laughs, no one cries;
Where he's gone, and how he fares,
No one knows, and no one cares.

Another:—

Here HENRY ROPER lies in dust;
His stature small, his mind was just.

Another, to the memory of MARGARET, the Wife of HUGH WRIGHT, is curious for its brevity and ingeniousness:—

(Eye) findeth; (Heart) chooseth; (Knot) bindeth; (Death) looseth.

The following epitaph was proposed to be placed in *Bath* Abbey :—

These walls, adorn'd with monumental bust,
Show how Bath waters serve to lay the dust.

In *Horsleydown* Church, *Cumberland :*—

Here lie the bodies
Of THOMAS BOND, and MARY his Wife.
She was temperate, chaste, and charitable;
But,
she was proud, peevish, and passionate.
She was an affectionate wife, and a tender mother;
But,
her husband and child, whom she loved,
seldom saw her countenance without a disgusting frown,
whilst she received visitors, whom she despised, with
an endearing smile.
Her behaviour was discreet towards strangers;
But,
imprudent in her family.
Abroad, her conduct was influenced by good breeding;
But,
at home, by ill temper.
She was a professed enemy to flattery,
and was seldom known to praise or commend;
But,
the talents in which she principally
excelled
were difference of opinion, and discovering
flaws and imperfections.
She was an admirable economist,

and, without prodigality,
dispensed plenty to every person in her family;
But
would sacrifice their eyes to a farthing candle.
She sometimes made her husband happy
with her good qualities;
But,
much more frequently miserable with
her many failings;
Insomuch, that in thirty years' cohabitation
he often lamented
that, maugre all her virtues,
he had not, in the whole, enjoyed two
years of matrimonial comfort.
At length,
finding she had lost the affection of her
husband, as well as the regard of her neighbours,
family disputes having been divulged by servants,
she died of vexation, *July* 20, 1768,
aged 48 years.
Her worn-out husband survived her four
months and two days,
and departed this life *Nov.* 28th, 1768,
in the 54th year of his age.
WILLIAM BOND, Brother to the deceased,
erected this stone
as a *weekly monitor* to the surviving
wives of this parish,
that they may avoid the infamy
of having their *memories* handed down to
posterity
with a patch-work character.

In a churchyard at *Cork :*—

> Here lies PAT STEELE,
> That's very true!
> Who was he? What was he?
> What's that to you?
> He lies here because he
> Is dead—nothing new!

On old JEREMIAH, who died in *Gray's Inn Lane* Workhouse :—

> Old JERRY's dead at last (God rest his soul),
> His body's shovell'd down some workhouse hole,
> Or else to Doctors given for dissection.
> His spirit's gone to Old Nick for correction,
> And his old clothes to spread some new infection!

In *Bampton, Devonshire :*—

> In memory of the clerk's son.
>
>> Bless my i, i, i, i, i, i,
>> Here I lies.
>> In a sad pickle,
>> Killed by icicle,
>
> In the year of *Anno Domini*, 1776.

In *Edwalton* Churchyard, *Notts.* Date, 1741. On Mrs. REBECCA FREELAND :—

> She drank good ale, strong punch, and wine,
> And lived to the age of ninety-nine.

Another :—

> Here lies poor THOMAS and his wife,
> Who led a pretty jarring life ;
> But all is ended—do you see,
> He holds his tongue, and so does she.

In a churchyard near *Folkestone:*—

This stone is sacread to the memory of poor old Muster THOMAS BOXER, who was loste in the goud boate Rouver, just coming home with much fishes, got near Torbay, in the year of hour Lord 1722.

> Pray, goud fishermen, stop and drop a tear,
> For we have lost his company *here,*
> And where he's gone we cannot tell,
> But we hope far from the wicked Bell.*

The Lord be with him.

Copied from the *San Diego Herald:*—

Here lies the body of JEEMS HUMBRICK
who was accidentally shot
on the bank of the pacus river
by a young man
he was accidentally shot with one of the large colt's revolver with no stopper for the cock to rest on it was one of the old fashion kind brass mounted and of such is the kingdom of heaven.

At *St. Lawrence's* Church, *Isle of Wight:*—

Sacred to the Memory of
WILLIAM JONES,
of Kensington Gore;
Who met his *untimely* death by an accident,
near this spot, on the 26th of *August,*
1826, in the 91st year
of his age.

---

* A public-house.

One choked with a bit of bread:—

> By many folks it hath been said,
> The only staff of life is bread,
> How could it then stop SIMON'S breath,
> And be the occasion of his death?
> One little morsel proved his last,
> Which he devour'd in so much haste,
> That angry Death in passion swore
> He ne'er should swallow one bit more.

In a churchyard in *Dorchester*:—

> FRANK from his Betty snatch'd by Fate
> Shows how uncertain-is our state.
> He smiled at morn—at noon lay dead,
> Flung from a horse that kick'd his head;
> But though he's gone, from tears refrain,
> At Judgment he'll get up again.

A *Highland* Epitaph:—

> Here lies interr'd a man of micht,
>   His name is MACOM DOWNIE;
> He lost his life one market nicht
>   By falling off his pownie.

On a fool who was shot through the head in a duel:—

> Here lies poor TOMMY; Nature at his end
> Thought 'twas but right for once to stand his friend;
> For in the shades below he now can say,
> "At least there's something in my head to-day."

On JOHN ROSS, *Jersey*:—

> Here lies JOHN ROSS,
> Kick'd by a hoss.

In a churchyard in *Staffordshire*, and hardly to be surpassed in terse and simple pathos :—

> This turf has drunk a widow's tear,
> Three of her husbands slumber here.

It may be interesting to state that the tearful widow was still living with a fourth partner.

In *Ballypooren* Churchyard. On TEAGUE O'BRIAN, written by himself :—

> Here I at length repose,
> My spirit now at aise is,
> With the tips of my toes
> And the point of my nose,
> Turn'd up to the roots of the daisies.

In the old Churchyard of *Belturbet, Ireland:*—

Here lies JOHN HIGLEY, whose father and mother were drowned on their passage from America. Had both *lived*, they would have been buried here!

In *Belbroughton* Churchyard, *Worcestershire*. On RICHARD PHILPOTS, of the Bell Inn, Bell End, who died in 1766 :—

> To tell a merry or a wondrous tale
> Over a cheerful glass of nappy ale,
> In harmless mirth was his supreme delight,
> To please his guests or friends by day or night.
> But no fine tale, how well soever told,
> Could make the tyrant Death his stroke withhold.
> That fatal stroke has laid him here in dust,
> To rise again once more with joy we trust.

On the upper portion of this monument are carved, in full relief, a punch bowl, a flagon, and a bottle, emblems of the deceased's faith (we presume), and of those pots which Mr. Philpots delighted to fill.

On Betsy Ooden:—

> Here lies Elizabeth
> Betsy Ooden,
> Her lived no longer
> Cos her—cooden.

Another:—

> The horse bit the parson!
> How came it to pass?
> The horse heard the parson say,
> "All flesh is grass."

Another:—

> An honest fellow here is laid,
> His debts in full he always paid;
> And, what's more strange, the neighbours tell us
> He brought back borrow'd umbrellas.

From *New Jersey:*—

> Weep, stranger, for a father spill'd
> From a stage coach, and thereby kill'd;
> His name was John Sykes, a maker of sassengers,
> Slain with three other outside passengers.

At *Portsmouth*, the following may be found on the tombstone of a carpenter, inscribed by his widow:—

> Here lies Jemmy Little, a carpenter industrious,
> A very good-natured man, but somewhat blusterous.
> When that his little wife his authority withstood,
> He took a little stick and bang'd her as he would.
> His wife, now left alone, her loss does so deplore,
> She wishes Jemmy back to bang her a little more;
> For now he's dead and gone this fault appears so small,
> A little thing would make her think it was no fault at all.

In *Creton* Churchyard, *Salop* :—

> On a Thursday she was born;
> On a Thursday made a bride;
> On a Thursday put to bed;
> On a Thursday broke her leg; and
> On a Thursday died.

Waltham Abbey, 1746 :—

> Your smiles I courte not,
> Nor your frowns I feare;
> My toils are ended;
> My head lies quiet here.

Same place :—

Too virtuous, kind, and just, with mortals to remain,
God thought fit, by the explosion of the mills, to take him back again.

Same place :—

> In the cold shades of night, lies prostrate here
> A loving husband, and a wife most dear;
> The first by sudden death did lead the way,
> And she by lightning quickly fell a prey.

At *St. Mary Overey, Borough.* On a stone under the arms of the Grocers' Company are these lines on one who followed that trade :—

> Weep not for him, he is gone before,
> To Heaven, where Grocers there are many more!

Same church. On SUSANNA BARFORD :—

> Such grace the King of kings bestow'd upon her,
> That now she lives with him a maid of honour!

In a churchyard near *Birmingham*:—

>Oh, cruel Death, why wert thou so unkind,
>To take the one, and leave the other behind?
>Thou shouldst have taken both or neither,
>Which would have been more agreeable to the survivor.

At *Richmond, Yorkshire*:—

>Here lies the body of WILLIAM WIX,
>One thousand, seven hundred, and sixty-six.

The following may be seen in a churchyard in *Essex*:—

>Weep not for me, my husband dear,
>Keep it in mind that I lies here,
>And have compassion on the nine
>Motherless children I left behind.

Another:—

>Underneath this turf doth lie,
>Back to back, my Wife and I.
>Generous stranger, spare the tear,
>For could she speak, I cannot hear.
>Happier far than when in life,
>Free from noise, and free from strife.
>When the last trump the air shall fill,
>If she gets up, I'll ev'n lie still.

At *Egam, North Derbyshire*:—

Here lise ye bodies of ANN SELLARS, buried by this stone, who died on *January* 13th day, 1731. Likewise here lise dear ISAAC SELLARS, my husband and my right, who was buried on that same day come seven years, 1738.

>In seven years' time there comes a change,
>Observe, and here you'll see,
>On that same day come seven years
>My husband's laid by me.

At *Bideford* Church, *Devon*:—

> The wedding day appointed was,
> And wedding clothes provided,
> And ere that day did come, alas!
> He sicken'd and he die did!

Grantham Churchyard, *Lincolnshire*:—

> JOHN PALFREYMAN, who lyeth here,
> Was aged four and twenty year;
> And near this place his mother lies,
> Also, his father, *when he dies!*

At *Wood Ditton*. On a gravestone in which is fixed an iron dish, according to the instructions of the deceased:—

> On WM. SYMONS, *ob.* 1753, *æt.* 80.
>
> Here lies my corpse, who was the man
> That loved a sop in the dripping pan;
> But now, believe me, I am dead,
> See how the pan stands at my head.
> Still for the sops till the last I cried,
> But could not eat, and so I died.
> My neighbours, they perhaps will laugh
> When they do read my epitaph.

At *Welshpool*:—

> Two lovely babes lie buried here,
> As ever bless'd their parents dear;
> But they were seized with ague fits,
> And here they lie as dead as nits.

In *Lillington* Churchyard:—

> I poorly lived; I poorly died;
> And when I was buried, nobody cried.

On a man named FISH:—

> Worms bait for fish; but here's a sudden change.
> *Fish* 's bait for worms—is not that passing strange?

On an infant three months old:—

> Since I am so quickly done for,
> I wonder what I was begun for.

On WILLIAM QUICK:—

> Here lies the quick and dead.

In *Banbury* Churchyard:—

> Here do lye our dear boy,
> Whom God hath tain from we,
> And we do hope that us shall go to he,
> For he can never come back again to we.

In a churchyard in *Sussex:*—

> In memory of Captain UNDERWOOD,
> who was drowned.

> Here lies free from blood and slaughter,
> Once *Underwood*—now under water.

Iver, Buckinghamshire. On R. CARTER:—

> An honest man; a friend sincere;
> What more can be said? He's buried here.

Edworth, Bedfordshire:—

> Here lies father, and mother, and sister, and I.
> We all died within the space of one year.
> They all be buried at Whimble, except I,
> And I be buried here.

In *Plymouth* Old Churchyard :—

> Here lies the body of
> THOMAS VERNON,
> The only *surviving* Son
> of
> Admiral VERNON.

In *Luton* Church :—

> Here lies the body of THOMAS PROCTOR,
> Who lived and died without a doctor.

In *St. Paul's, Covent Garden* :—

On Mr. JAMES WORSDALE, Painter and Author, composed by himself :—

> Eager to get, but not to keep the pelf,
> A friend to all mankind—except himself.

In *Marnhall* Churchyard, *Dorsetshire*. On a tomb erected to the memory of ROBERT and MARY MOORE, and their daughter FRANCES, dated 1670 :—

> See what Death with 's spade hath done to wee,
> Having new planted both bud, branch, and tree.

On a Miss LONG, a most beautiful young lady :—

> Though long, yet short,
> Though short, yet *pretty* long.

At *St. Alban's* :—

> Sacred to the memory of Miss MARTHA GWYNN,
> Who was so very pure within,
> She burst the outer shell of sin,
> And hatch'd herself a cherubim.

In a cemetery near *Salisbury*. On RICHARD BUTTON:—

> Oh! Sun, Moon, Stars, and ye celestial Poles,
> Are graves then dwindled into *Button-holes?*

Brighton Old Churchyard :—

> His fate was hard, but God's decree,
> Was drown'd he should be in the sea.

In *Watton* Churchyard, *Norfolk* :—

> Underneath this sod lies JOHN ROUND,
> Who was lost in the sea, and never was found.

At the same place :—

> Here lies MATTHEW MUD. Death did him no hurt,
> When alive he was *Mud*, and now dead he's but dirt.

Another :—

> Here lies, cut down like unripe fruit,
> The wife of Master AMOS SHUTE,
> She died of drinking too much coffee,
> Anno Domini Eighteen Forty.

In *Hackney* Churchyard. On one PETER STILLER :—

> As still as Death poor Peter lies,
> And *Stiller* when alive was he,
> Still not without a hope to rise,
> Though *Stiller* then he still will be.

At *Bury St. Edmund's,* and at *Painswick, Gloucestershire* :—

> Here lies JANE HITCHEN, who when her glass was spent,
> Kickt up her heels, and away she went.

Strange Epitaph :—

The following inscription is actually to be found in an ancient cemetery in *Rockville* Eastern *Massachusetts* :—

> In memory of JANE BENT,
> Who kick'd up her heels and away she went.

At *Massachusetts, America* :—

> I came in the morning—it was Spring,
>   And I smiled ;
> I walk'd out at noon—it was Summer,
>   And I was glad ;
> I sat me down at even—it was Autumn,
>   And I was sad ;
> I laid me down at night—it was Winter,
>   And I slept.

In *Stepney* Churchyard :—

> Here THOMAS SAPPER lies interr'd, Ah why ?
> Born in New England, did in London die ;
> Was the third son of eight, begot upon
> His mother Martha, by his father John ;
> Much favour'd by his Prince he 'gan to be,
> But nipt by death at the age of twenty-three.
> Fatal to him was that we small-pox name,
> By which his mother and two brethren came
> Also to breathe their last, nine years before,
> And now have left their father to deplore
> The loss of all his children, with his wife,
> Who was the joy and comfort of his life.

Same place :—

Here lieth R. CROUCH, in expectation of the last day. What sort of a man he was, that day will discover.

Epitaph in a *Cornish* Churchyard :—

> In this ere graave ee zee bevore ee,
> Is berred up a desmal stoery
> A young maiden she wor crost in love
> And tooken to the realms above
> But he that crost her I shud zay
> Desarves to go the toyther way.

On THOMAS HUDDLESTONE :—

Here lies THOMAS HUDDLESTONE. Reader, don't smile,
But reflect, as this tombstone you view,
That Death, who kill'd him, in a very short while
Will *huddle a stone* upon you.

At *Cheltenham* :—

> Here lies I and my three daughters,
> Kill'd by drinking the Cheltenham waters ;
> If we had stuck to our Epsom salts,
> We'd not been a lying in these here vaults.

Sevenoaks Churchyard, *Kent* :—

Grim Death took me without any warning,
I was well at night, and dead at nine in the morning.

At *Dijon.* On LE MENESTRIER :—

> JEAN LE MENESTRIER lieth here :
> Lo! having number'd his seventieth year,
> He tightens his stirrups, his spurs he plies,
> And starts away for Paradise.

At *Bideford, Devon* :—

Here lie two brothers, by misfortune surrounded,
One died of his wounds, and the other was drownded.

On William Willing :—

> Death will'd that *Willing* here should lie,
> Although *unwilling* he to die.

Westminster Abbey. On Ephraim Chambers (by himself) :—

> Heard of by many,
> Known to few,
> Who led a Life between Fame and Obscurity,
> Neither abounding nor deficient in Learning,
> Devoted to Study, but as a Man
> Who thinks himself bound to all Offices of Humanity,
> Having finished his Life and his Labour together,
> Here desires to rest,
> Ephraim Chambers,
> *Obiit* May 15th, 1740.

On Thomas Crabtree, 1860 :—

> Short was my stay in this vain world,
> All but a seeming laughter ;
> Therefore mark well my words and ways,
> For thou com'st posting after.

Another, dated 1672, to the memory of George Jackson, is certainly more loyal than religious :—

> To King and State, in spite of fate,
> I have been true and just ;
> For all which pain I shall obtain
> A crown that shall not rust.

Not more satisfactory is the following :—

> Here lies the body of John Drake,
> Who never did his friend forsake ;

Houses and land he left to be
A free schoolmaster's salary ;
He lived and died without a mate,
And yielded to the laws of fate.

The following conveys a poor compliment to the deceased's husband :—

MARIA BROWN, wife of TIMOTHY BROWN, aged eighty years. She lived with her husband fifty years, and died in the confident hope of a better life.

Another reads thus :—

Here lies BERNARD LIGHTFOOT, who was accidentally killed in the forty-fifth year of his age. This monument was erected by his *grateful* family.

There is a tablet in a churchyard in *Haddingtonshire, Scotland*, professed to be erected by a sorrowing husband to his wife as a testimony of his *filial* regard.

In *Homersfield* Churchyard, *Suffolk*. On ROBERT CRYTOFT, died 1810, aged 90 :—

> As I walk'd by myself, I talk'd to myself,
>   And thus myself said to me:
> Look to thyself, and take care of thyself,
>   For nobody cares for thee.
>
> So I turn'd to myself, and I answer'd myself,
>   In the self-same reverie :
> Look to thyself, or look not to thyself,
>   The self-same thing will be.

In the Churchyard of *Dunkeld*. On MARGERY SCOTT,

who lived single 25 years, married 50 years, and was a widow 50 years, died 1738 :—

> Stop, reader, here, until my life you've read.
> The living may gain knowledge from the dead;
> Five times five years I've lived a virgin's life,
> Ten times five years I was a married wife;
> Ten times five years a widow grave and chaste;
> Now, wearied of this mortal life I rest.
> I from my cradle to my grave have seen
> Eight mighty kings of Scotland and a queen;
> Four times five years the Commonwealth I saw,
> Ten times the subjects rise against the law;
> Twice did I see old prelacy put down,
> And twice the cloak did sink beneath the gown:
> An end of Stuart's race I saw,—nay, more,
> I saw my country sold for English ore;
> Such dissolution in my time has been,
> That I've an end of all perfection seen.

In *Nayland* Churchyard, *Suffolk :*—

> Here sleepeth in dust,
> NED ALSTON,
> The notorious Essex Highwayman,
> *Ob. Anno Dom.* 1760.
> *Ætat* 40.

> My friends, here I am—Death at last has prevail'd,
>   And for once all my projects are baffled,
> 'Tis a blessing to know, tho', when once a man's *nail'd,*
>   He has no further dread of the scaffold.

> My life was cut short by a shot thro' the head,
>   On his Majesty's highway at Dalston—
> So as now ' Number One ' 's numbered one of the dead,
>   All's one *if* he's *Alston* or *All-stone.*

Another :—

> Hope, fear, false joy, and trouble,
> Are the four winds which daily toss this bubble.
> His breath's a vapour, and his life's a span.
> 'Tis glorious misery to be born a man.

Another in *Milton* Churchyard, *Kent*, and in *Bengeo* Old Churchyard, *Hertfordshire* :—

> This world's a city full of crooked streets ;
> Death is the market-place where each one meets.
> If life were only merchandize to buy,
> The rich would live—the poor alone would die.

Dirge to the memory of Miss ELLEN GEE, of *Kew*, who died in consequence of being stung in the eye :—

> Peerless yet hapless maid of Q,
>   Accomplish'd L N G,
> Never again shall I and U
>   Together sip our T.
>
> For, ah! the Fates, I know not Y,
>   Sent 'midst the flowers a B,
> Which ven'mous stung her in the I,
>   So that she could not C.
>
> L. N. exclaim'd, Vile spiteful B,
>   If ever I catch U
> On jess'mine, rosebud, or sweet P,
>   I'll change your stinging Q.
>
> I'll send you, like a lamb or U,
>   Across the Atlantic C,
> From our delightful village Q,
>   To distant O Y E.
>
> A stream runs from my wounded I,
>   Salt as the briny C,
> As rapid as the X or Y,
>   The O I O or D.
>
> Then fare-thee-well, insatiate B,
>   Who stung, nor yet knew Y,
> Since not for wealthy Durham's C
>   Would I have lost my I.
>
> They bear with tears fair L N G.
>   In funeral R A,
> A clay-cold corse now doom'd to B,
>   While I mourn her D K.
>
> Ye nymphs of Q, then shun each B,
>   List to the reason Y :
> For should a B C U at T,
>   He'll surely sting your I.
>
> Now in a grave L deep in Q,
>   She's cold as cold can B,
> Whilst robins sing upon A U
>   Her dirge and L E G.

In *Broom* Churchyard the following Epitaph may be seen :—

In memory of
JOSEPH and WALTER DUDLEY, Brothers,
Both of this Parish,
Who left this for a better world,
Jan. 18, 1797. *Anno Ætat,* $\begin{cases} 18. \\ 15. \end{cases}$

Reader, beneath this tombstone moulder
    The trunks of Joe and Wat ;
Wat, youngest ; Joe, the elder ;
    Joe, lean ; and Walter, fat.

Till late these youngters were of *Broom*,
    But Wednesday last 'twas found
That death from *Broom* had made them *brush*,
    And *swept* them under ground.

In *Beckley* Church, and also in *Newport* Churchyard, *Gloucestershire*, (written by Swift) :—

Here lies the Earl of Suffolk's fool,
    Men called him DICKY PEARCE ;
His folly served to make folk's laugh,
    When wit and mirth were scarce.

Poor Dick, alas ! is dead and gone,
    What signifies to cry?
Dickies enough are left behind
    To laugh at by-and-by.

At *Ditchington* Churchyard :—

Without a home for ever, senseless, dumb,
Dust only now contains this silent tomb.
Where 'twas I lived or died, it matters not ;
To whom related, or of whom begot.

> I was, but am not: ask no more of me ;
> 'Tis all I am, and all that you must be.

On a tombstone in *New Jersey* is the following significant epitaph :—

JULIA ADAMS,

Died of thin shoes, April 17th, 1839, aged 19 years.

If the truth were always spoken, there would be many epitaphs of the same description.

At *Wolstanton* :—

> Some have children, some have none ;
> Here lies the mother of twenty-one.

On an epicure :—

> At length, my friends, the feast of life is o'er :
> I've eat sufficient—I can drink no more.
> My night is come ; I've spent a jovial day:
> 'Tis time to part—but, oh! what is to pay?

In *Merrow* Church, *Surrey* :—

In memory of SARAH BATTAY, wife of THOMAS BATTAY, who died the 6th of June, 1799, aged 103 years.

> By *St. David's* rule our ages then
> Were number'd threescore years and ten ;
> But if to fourscore years we gain,
> Our labour then but grief and pain.
> At ninety years I do depend
> To make a good and holy end ;
> But at one hundred years and three
> The grave's the bed that best suits me.

The two next epitaphs relate to *Fees,* and are curious compositions :—

Chart-Magna Church, *Kent :—*

In memory of ANN WEST, widow, of this parish, died March 10, 1800, aged 59 years,

> The Reverend Rector being a hard
> Austerely rigid man,
> Within the walls of this churchyard
> He will not let me stand,
> Unless a fee be paid to him,
> Two shillings and two pounds,
> So to the memory of a friend
> I here am now set down.

At *West Allington, Devon :—*

> Here lyeth the Body of DANIEL JEFFREY,
> the son of Michael Jeffrey and Joan his Wife.
> He was buried ye 22 day of September, 1746,
> in ye 18th year of his age.

> This Youth, When In his sickness lay,
> did for the Minister send, × that he would
> Come and With him Pray, × But he would not atend ;
> But when this young man Buried was
> The Minister did him admit × he should be
> Carried into Church, × that he might money geet:
> By this you See what man will dwo × to geet
> money if he can, × who did refuse to come
> and pray × by the Foresaid young man.

In the Niew Kirk, at *Amsterdam,* is a very ancient monument, on which a pair of slippers of a singular kind are carved, with this inscription : "*Effen Nyt,*" which means "*exactly,*" and the story of this singularity is as follows :—

WITTY AND GROTESQUE.

A man who was very rich, but who was a *bon vivant*, took it into his head that he was to live a certain number of years, and no longer. Under the impression of this idea, he calculated that if he spent so much a year, his estate and his life would expire together. It accidentally happened that he was not mistaken in either of his calculations; he died precisely at the time he had fancied he would, and had then brought his fortune to such a predicament that, after the paying of his debts, he had nothing left but a pair of slippers. His relations buried him in a creditable manner, and had the slippers carved on his tomb with the above laconic epitaph.

In *High Wycombe* Churchyard. On Mr. THOMAS ALDRIDGE, aged 90 :—

>Of no distemper,
>Of no blast he died,
>But fell,
>Like autumn fruit
>That's mellow'd long,
>E'en wonder'd at,
>Because he dropt no sooner.
>Providence seem'd to wind him up
>For fourscore years, yet ran he on
>Nine winters more, till like a clock,
>Worn out with beating time,
>At last stood still.

Inscription over the grave of a Fifer :—

>*Hic Jacet*
>1 ... 5 - 4,
>0 ... 4 ... 1 ... 2 ... 8,
>0 ... 4 ... 1 ... 2 ... 0,
>0 ... 2 ... 80 ... 8,
>0 ... 2 ... 45 ... 4.

This means—

> Here lies
> One Fifer.
> Nought for one to wait,
> Nought for one to sigh for,
> Nought to weighty ate,
> Nought to fortify for.

On MARTHA SNELL, and a similar one in *Staverton* Churchyard :—

> Poor MARTHA SNELL! her's gone away,
> Her would if her could, but her couldn't stay;
> Her'd two sore legs, and a badish cough,
> But her legs it was as carried her off.

On Mrs. DEATH :—

> Here lies Death's wife: when this way next you tread,
> Be not surprised should Death himself be dead.

On an actor named DEATH :—

> Death levels all, both high and low,
> Without regard to stations;
> Yet why complain
> If *we* are slain?
> For here lies one at least to show
> He kills his own relations.

At St. Mary's Church, *Shrewsbury*, JOHN CADMAN lies buried; he was killed in an attempt to fly from the spire (217 feet) in 1740. On a flat stone near the west door are the following lines :—

> Let this small monument record the name
> Of CADMAN, and to future times proclaim

How by'n attempt to fly from this high spire,
Across the Sabrine stream, he did acquire
His fatal end. 'Twas not for want of skill
Or courage to perform the task he fell:
No, no ; a faulty cord, being drawn too tight,
Hurried his soul on high to take her flight,
Which hid the body here beneath. Good-night.

Under which some rhymester once wrote :—

Good-night, good-night, poor JOHN CADMAN,
You lived and died just like a madman.

In *Cirencester* Churchyard, *Gloucestershire* :—

Our bodies are like shoes, which off we cast ;
Physic their cobblers ; and Death their last.

On a celebrated ruling elder, by Robert Burns :—

Here souter HOOD in death does sleep—
  To hell, if he's gane thither,
Satan, gie him thy gear to keep,
  He'll haud it weel thegither.

By the same :—

Hic jacet wee Johnnie.

Whoe'er thou art, O reader, know,
  That death has murder'd JOHNNY,
An' here his body lies fu' low—
  For saul he ne'er had ony.

By the same :—

Here lies, now a prey to insulting neglect,
  What once was a butterfly gay in life's beam ;
Want only of wisdom denied her respect,
  Want only of goodness denied her esteem.

By the same :—

>Here Holy WILLIE'S sair-worn clay
>   Taks up its last abode;
>His soul has ta'en some other way,
>   I fear the left-hand road.
>
>Stop! there he is, as sure 's a gun,
>   Poor, silly body, see him;
>Nae wonder he's as black 'as the grun',
>   Observe wha's standing wi' him.
>
>Your brunstane devilship, I see,
>   Has got him there before ye;
>But haud your nine-tail cat a wee,
>   Till ance you've heard my story.
>
>Your pity I will not implore,
>   For pity ye hae nane :
>Justice, alas! has gi'en him o'er,
>   And Mercy's day is gaen.
>
>But hear me, sir, deil as ye are,
>   Look something to your credit;
>A coof like him wad stain your name,
>   If it were kent ye did it.

The following may be seen in a churchyard in the parish of *Eskdalemuir, Dumfries* :—

>Here lies JOHN LAURIE,
>   Neither rich nor poor,
>Last minister of Wauchoppe,
>   And first of Eskdalemuir.

On RICHARD BURKE :—

>Here lies honest RICHARD, whose fate I must sigh at;
>Alas, that such frolic should now be so quiet!
>What spirits were his! what wit and what whim!
>Now breaking a jest, and now breaking a limb!

Now wrangling and grumbling to keep up the ball!
Now teasing and vexing, yet laughing at all!
In short, so provoking a fellow was Dick,
That we wish'd him full ten times a day at Old Nick;
But missing his mirth and agreeable vein,
As often we wish'd to have Dick back again!

At *Edinburgh* :—

Here lies JOHN and his Wife,
JANET MCFEE,
40 hee—30 shee.

On THOMAS KEMP, a woolcomber, who was hanged for sheep-stealing :—

Here lies the body of THOMAS KEMP,
Who *lived* by wool, but *died* by hemp;
There's nothing would suffice this glutton,
But, with the fleece, to steal the mutton.
Had he but work'd and lived uprighter,
He'd ne'er been hung for a sheep-biter.

In *Wrexham* Churchyard :—

RICHARD KENDRICK was buried August 29th, 1785, by *the desire of his wife*, Margaret Kendrick.

At *St. Bennet's, Paul's Wharf, London* :—

Here lies one *More*, and no more than he,
One *More* and no more—how can that be?
Why one *More* and no more may well lie here alone;
But here lies one *More*, and that's more than one.

Another :—

Here old JOHN RANDELL lies, who, telling of his tale,
Lived threescore years and ten, such virtue was in ale:
Ale was his meat; ale was his drink; ale did his heart revive;
And if he could have drunk his ale, he still had been alive.

On an Attorney :—

>Here lies JOHN SHAW,
>Attorney-at-law ;
>And when he died,
>The Devil cried,
>" Give us your paw,
>JOHN SHAW
>Attorney-at-law !"
>"Pshaw! pshaw."

In *Worcester* Churchyard :—

>Mammy and I together lived
> Just two years and a half;
>She went first—I followed next,
> The cow before the calf.

On a Punster :—

>Beneath the gravel and these stones,
>Lies poor JACK TIFFEY'S skin and bones;
>His flesh I oft have heard him say,
>He hoped in time would make good hay;
>Quoth I, "How can that come to pass?"
>And he replied, "All flesh is grass!"

On a tombstone in *Essex* :—

>Here lies the man RICHARD,
> And MARY his wife,
>Their surname was PRICHARD ;
> They lived without strife,
>And the reason was plain—
> They abounded in riches ;
>They had no care, nor pain,
> And the wife wore the breeches.

On WILLIAM WILSON, tailor, in *Lambeth* Churchyard :—

>Here lies the body of W. W.,
>Who never more will trouble you, trouble you.

On a Smuggler :—

>Here I lies,
>Kill'd by the X I S.

In *Wolverhampton* Church, *Ob.* 1690 :—

>Here lies the bones
>Of JOSEPH JONES,
>Who ate whilst he was able;
>But, once o'erfed,
>He dropt down dead,
>And fell beneath the table.
>When from the tomb,
>To meet his doom,
>He rises amidst sinners;
>Since he must dwell
>In heaven or hell,
>Take him—which gives best dinners!

At *Chester*. On a Sexton :—

>Hurra! my brave boys, let's rejoice at his fall!
>For if he had lived, he had buried us all.

On ISAAC REED, by Thomas Dibdin :—

>Reader, of these four lines take heed,
>And mend your life for my sake;
>For you must die, like ISAAC REED,
>Tho' you *read* till your *eyes ache!*

On an Innkeeper :—

Hark! hark ye, old friend! what! will pass then without
  Taking notice of honest plump Jack?
You see how"'tis with me, my light is burnt out,
  And they've laid me here flat on my back.

That light in my nose, once so bright to behold,
  That light is extinguish'd at last ;
And I'm now put to bed in the dark and the cold,
  With wicker and so forth made fast.
But now, wilt oblige me? then call for a quart
  Of the best, from the house o'er the way ;
Drink a part on't thyself, on my grave pour a part,
  And walk on,—Friend, I wish thee good-day.

Another :—

  Assign'd by Providence to rule a tap,
  My days pass'd glibly, till an awkward rap,
  Some way, like bankruptcy, impell'd me down,
  But up I got again, and shook my gown
  In gamesome gambols, quite as brisk as ever,
  Blithe as the lark, and gay as sunny weather ;
  Composed with creditors, at five in pound,
  And frolick'd on till laid beneath this ground.
  The debt of Nature must, you know, be paid,
  No trust from her—God grant *extent in aid !*

At *Frindsbury, Kent.* On Mrs. LEE and her son TOM :—

  In her life she did her best,
  Now I hope her soul's at rest ;
  Also her son TOM lies at her feet—
  He lived till he made both ends meet !

On a scolding woman :—

  We lived one and twenty yeare,
    Like man and wife together ;
  I could no longer have her here,
    She's gone—I know not whither.
  If I could guess, I doe professe
    (I speak it not to flatter),
  Of all the women in the worlde,
    I never could come at her !

> Her body is bestowed well,
>   A handsome grave doth hide her;
> And sure her soul is not in hell—
>   The Fiend could nere abide her!
> I think she mounted up on high,
>   For in the last great thunder,
> Methought I heard her voice on high,
>   Rending the clouds in sunder.

On a quarrelsome man:—

> Beneath this stone lies one whose life
> Was spent in quarrels and in strife.
> Wake not his spirit from its rest,
> For when he slept the world was blest.

Teetotaller's Epitaph. In the *European Magazine* for March, 1796, there is this "epitaph" on a water-drinker:—

> Here lies NED RAND, who on a sudden,
> Left off roast beef for hasty pudding:
> Forsook old stingo, mild and stale,
> And every drink for Adam's ale;
> Till flesh and blood reduced to batter,
> Consisting of mere flour and water,
> Which, wanting salt to keep out must,
> And heat to bake it to a crust,
> Moulder'd and crumbled into dust.

On Sir WILLIAM CURTIS:—

> Here lies WILLIAM CURTIS, late our Lord Mayor,
> Who has left *this here* world and gone to *that there*.

On Captain STONE:—

> As the earth the earth doth cover,
> So under this stone lies another.

In *St. John's* Church, *Chester*. On a swift-footed man :—

> Here lies the swift racer, so famed for his running,
> In spite of his boasting, his swiftness, and cunning ;
> In leaping o'er ditches, and skipping o'er fields,
> Death soon overtook him, and tript up his heels.

In *Thetford* Churchyard :—

> My grandfather lies buried here,
> My cousin Jane, and two uncles dear ;
> My father perish'd with inflammation in the thighs,
> And my sister dropt down dead in the Minories.
> But the reason I'm here interr'd, according to my thinking,
> Is owing to my good living and hard drinking ;
> If therefore, good Christians, you wish to live long,
> Don't drink too much wine, brandy, gin, or anything strong.

On Sir NATHANIEL WRAXALL, written by George Colman the younger :—

> Misplacing—mistaking—
> Misquoting—misdating—
> Men, manners, things, and facts all—
> Here lies Sir NATHAN WRAXALL.

At *Brightwell, Oxon*. On S. RUMBOLD, born Feb., 1582 :—

> He lived one hundred and five,
>   Sanguine and strong ;
> A hundred to five
>   You live not so long.

Dy'd March 4, 1687.

At *Herne Bay* Churchyard :—

> Here lie two children dear,
> One at Margate, and two here.

At *St. Agnes, Cornwall* :—

> Here lies the body of JOAN CARTHEW,
> Born at Saint Columb, died at St. Cue;
> Children she had five,
> Three are dead, and two alive;
> Those that are dead chusing rather
> To die with their mother, than live with their father.

At *Tavistock, Devon* :—

> Under this stone lies three children dear,
> Two be buried at Tawton, and the other here.

At *Herne Bay* Churchyard :—

> Here lie two children dear:
> One at Margate and two here.

On Mr. ALEXANDER SPEID, in the *Houff, Dundee* :—

> Time flies with speed, with speed Speid's fled
> To the dark regions of the dead;
> With speed consumption's sorrows flew,
> And stopt Speid's speed, for Speid it slew:
> Miss Speid beheld, with frantic woe,
> Poor Speid with speed turn pale as snow,
> And beat her breast and tore her hair,
> For Speid, poor Speid, was all her care.
> Let's learn of Speid with speed to fly
> From sin, since we like Speid must die.

At *High Wycombe, Bucks* :—

> Death is a fisherman; the world we see
> A fishpond is, and we the fishes be;
> He sometimes angler-like doth with us play,
> And slily takes us one by one away.

At *Acton, Gloucester* :—

> Here lies entomb'd one ROGER MORTON,
> Whose sudden death was early brought on ;
> Trying one day his corn to mow off,
> The razor slipt and cut his toe off ;
> The toe, or rather what it grew to,
> An inflammation quickly flew to ;
> The parts they took to mortifying,
> And poor dear Roger took to dying.

On a wife :—

> I laid my wife beneath this stone
> For her repose and for my own.

On a clergyman named CHEST :—

> Here lies at rest, I do protest,
>   One Chest within another ;
> The chest of wood was very good—
>   Who says so of the other?

On a great eater :—

> Whoe'er you are, tread softly, I entreat you ;
> For if he chance to wake, be sure he'll eat you.

On a hen-pecked country squire :—

> As father Adam first was fool'd,
>   A case that's still too common,
> Here lies a man a woman ruled—
>   The devil ruled the woman.

In *Eccleston* Churchyard, near *Chester*. On JOHN HUXLEY :—

> Poor Jack, he lies beneath this rood,
> And sure he must be blest,

>   For if he could do nothing good,
>   He meant to do his best.
>   Think on your souls, ye guilty throng,
>   Who, knowing what is right, does wrong.

On Mr. PECK :—

>   Here lies a Peck, which some men say,
>   Was first of all a Peck of clay ;
>   This, wrought with skill divine, while fresh,
>   Became a curious Peck of flesh :
>   Through various forms its Maker ran,
>   Then, adding breath, made Peck a man.
>   Full sixty years Peck felt life's bubbles,
>   Till Death relieved a Peck of troubles ;
>   Thus fell poor Peck, as all things must,
>   And here he lies—a Peck of dust.

On Captain JONES, a great traveller and story-teller :—

>   Tread softly, mortals, o'er the bones
>   Of the world's wonder, Captain JONES ;
>   Who told his glorious deeds to many,
>   But never was believed by any.
>   Posterity, let this suffice :
>   He swore all's true, yet here he *lies.*

At *Ancrum Moor, Roxburgh, Scotland.* On MAIDEN LILLIARD, who at the battle of Ancrum distinguished herself :—

Fair MAIDEN LILLIARD lies under this stone :
Little was her stature, but great was her fame ;
Upon the English lions she had laid many thumps,
And when her legs were cutted off she fought upon her stumps.

Some years since the following inscription, engraved on a stone, was discovered amongst the relics of an antiquarian, and considered a great curiosity by its translation having puzzled scholars :—

>   Bene
>   A. T. H. TH. ISST.
>   onere . Pos . ET .
>   H CLAUD COS TER . TRIP
>   E . SELLERO
>   F. IMP
>   IN . GT . ONAS DO
>   TH . HI
>   S . C
>   ON . S OR
>   T . IANE.

Some supposed it to refer to the Emperor CLAUDIAN, till one day a lad spelled it out :—

Beneath this stone reposeth CLAUD COSTER, tripe-seller, of *Impington*, as doth his consort JANE.

In *Barrow-on-Soar* Church, *Leicestershire*. On THEOPHILUS CAVES, 1584 :—

> Here in this Grave there lies a *Cave*
>   We call a *Cave* a Grave ;
> If *Cave* be Grave, and Grave be *Cave*,
>   Then, reader, judge, I crave,
> Whether doth *Cave* here lye in Grave,
>   Or Grave here lye in *Cave* :
> If Grave in *Cave* here buryed lye,
>   Then Grave, where is thy victory ?
> Goe, reader ! and report,
>   Here lies a *Cave*
> Who conquers Death,
>   And buryes his own Grave.

On the Marquis of ANGLESEA'S leg :—

> Here lies,—and let no saucy knave
>   Presume to sneer or laugh,
> To learn that mould'ring in this cave
>   Is laid a British *calf*.
> For he who writes these lines is sure
>   That those who read the whole,
> Would find that laugh were premature,
>   For here, too, lies a *sole*.
> And here five little ones repose,
>   Twin born with other five,
> Unheeded by their brother toes,
>   Who now are all alive.
> A leg and foot, to speak more plain,
>   Rest here of one commanding ;
> And tho' his wits he may retain,
>   Lost half his *understanding*:
> Who, when the guns, with thunder fraught,
>   Pour'd bullets thick as hail,
> Could only in this way be brought
>   To give the foe *leg-bail* ;
> And now in England, just as gay
>   As in the battle brave,
> Goes to the rout, review, or play,
>   With one foot in the grave.
> Fortune, indeed, has shown her spite,
>   (For he will still be found,
> Should England's foes engage in fight,
>   Resolved to stand his ground,)
> And but indulged in harmless whim,
>   Since he could walk with one,
> She saw two legs were lost on him,
>   Who never deign'd to run.

An inscription on a stone, within a niche in the wall of the mausoleum in Lord Cobham's garden at *Stow* :—

To the memory of
Signor FIDO,
An Italian of good Extraction,
Who came into England,
Not to *bite* us, like most of his Countrymen,
But to gain an honest Livelyhood.
He *hunted* not after Fame,
Yet acquired it.
Regardless of the Praise of his Friends,
But most sensible of their Love.
Tho' he lived among the Great,
He neither learnt nor flatter'd any Vice.
He was no Bigot,
Tho' he doubted of none of the Thirty-nine
Articles :
And if to follow Nature,
And to respect the Laws of Society,
Be Philosophy ;
He was a perfect Philosopher,
A faithful Friend,
An agreeable Companion,
A loving Husband;
And, tho' an Italian,
Was distinguished by a numerous Offspring :
All which he liv'd to see take good Courses.
In his old Age he retir'd
To the house of a Clergyman in the Country,
Where he finish'd his *earthly Race*,
And died an Honour and Example to the
whole species.
Reader,
This Stone is guiltless of Flattery ;

> For he to whom it was inscrib'd
> Was not a Man,
> But a Grey Hound.

On the monument of a Newfoundland Dog, in the garden of *Newstead*, by Lord Byron :—

> Near this spot
> Are deposited the Remains of one
> Who possessed Beauty without Vanity,
> Strength without Insolence,
> Courage without Ferocity,
> And all the Virtues of Man without his Vices.
> This Praise, which would be unmeaning Flattery
> If inscribed over human ashes,
> Is but a just tribute to the Memory of
> BOATSWAIN, a Dog,
> Who was born at *Newfoundland, May*, 1803,
> And died at *Newstead* Abbey, *Nov.* 18, 1808.

> When some proud son of man returns to earth,
> Unknown to glory, but upheld by birth,
> The sculptor's art exhausts the pomp of woe,
> And storied urns record who rest below ;
> When all is done, upon the tomb is seen,
> Not what he was, but what he should have been :
> But the poor dog, in life the firmest friend,
> The first to welcome, foremost to defend,
> Whose honest heart is still his master's own,
> Who labours, fights, lives, breathes for him alone,
> Unhonour'd falls, unnoticed all his worth,
> Denied in heaven the soul he held on earth :
> While man, vain insect ! hopes to be forgiven,
> And claims himself a sole exclusive heaven.
> Oh man ! thou feeble tenant of an hour,
> Debased by slavery, or corrupt by power,

Who knows thee well must quit thee with disgust,
Degraded man of animated dust.
Thy love is lust, thy friendship all a cheat,
Thy smiles hypocrisy, thy words deceit!
By nature vile, ennobled but by name,
Each kindred brute might bid thee blush for shame.
Ye, who perchance behold this simple urn,
Pass on—it honours none you wish to mourn:
To mark a friend's remains these stones arise;
I never knew but one—and here he lies.

Singular Inscription :—

No monument that we are aware of has ever been erected to the memory of a pig. The town of *Lunenburg*, in *Hanover*, has filled up that blank, and at the *Hotel de Ville*, in that town, there is to be seen a kind of mausoleum to the memory of a member of the swinish race. In the interior of that commemorative structure is to be seen a glass-case, enclosing a ham still in good preservation. A slab of black marble attracts the eye of visitors, who find thereon the following inscription in Latin, engraved in letters of gold : " Passer-by, contemplate here the mortal remains of the pig which acquired for itself imperishable glory by the discovery of the salt springs of *Lunenburg*.

IV.

Miscellaneous Epitaphs.

St. Ann's, Aldersgate. On PETER HEIWOOD :—

PETER HEIWOOD,
Youngest son of Peter Heiwood,
One of the Counsellors of *Jamaica*,
By Grace, Daughter of Sir John Muddeford,
Knt. and Bart.,
Great Grandson to Peter Heiwood, of *Heiwood*,
In the County Palatine of *Lancaster*,
Who apprehended Guy Faux
With his dark Lanthorn,
And for his zealous Prosecution of Papists,
As Justice of the Peace,
Was stabbed in *Westminster* Hall,
By John James, a *Dominican* Fryar,
Anno Dom. 1640.
Obiit Nov. 2, 1701.

On EDWARD MORGAN, who died in 1828, at *Saint Bride's Minor, Glamorganshire* :—

> O Earth ! O Earth ! observe this well,
> That earth to earth must come to dwell ;
> Then earth in earth shall close remain,
> Till earth from earth shall rise again.

In *Burford* Church, *Shropshire*, is a handsome monument to the memory of ELIZABETH, daughter of John of Gaunt, and sister to Henry IV.

At *Frodsham* Church, *Cheshire*, was buried, March 13, 1592, THOMAS HOUGH, aged 141, and the very next day RANDLE HALL, aged 103.

On a brass tablet in *Willaston* Chapel, *Shropshire* :—

> The Old, Old, very Old Man,
> THOMAS PARR,
> Was born at the Glyn
> within this Chapelry of *Great Willaston*,
> and Parish of *Alberbury*,
> in the County of *Salop*,
> In the Year of our Lord, 1483.
> He lived in the Reigns of Ten Kings
> and Queens of *England* (viz.) K. Edw : 4,
> K. Edwd. 5, K. Rich. 3, K. Hen. 7th, K. Hen. 8th,
> Edwd. 6th, Q. Mary, Q. Elizabeth, K. James 1st, and
> K. Charles 1st, died the 13th,
> And was buried in *Westminster* Abbey,
> On the 15th of November, 1635,
> Aged 152 years and 9 months.

The inscription in *Westminster* Abbey is very similar to the above.

At a place called *Kirkmichael*, in the *Isle of Man*, and in the churchyard of that place, is an upright stone, of great antiquity, on which are chiselled various devices of horse-riders, dogs, and stags; on the upper part is a warrior, with a spear and shield; on the edge are some runic characters, which are thus variously translated by different antiquarians. Sir John Prestwich asserts that the words form the following sentence: " Walter, son of Thurulf, a Knight, right valiant, Lord of Frithu, the Father, Jesus Christ." Whereas Mr. Beaufort, with equal confidence, reads the inscription thus: " For the sins of Ivalsir, the son of Duval, this cross was erected by his mother, Aftridi."

In an old volume containing the History of FAIR ROSAMOND, daughter of Lord Clifford, and mistress to Henry II., it is stated that the King caused a stately tomb to be erected to her memory at *Godstow*, near *Oxford*, on which was this inscription in Latin:—

> Within this tomb lies the world's chiefest Rose,
> She who was sweet will now offend your nose.

From *Hothfield* Churchyard, *Kent*:—

CHARLOTTE SPARKS was my name; England was my nation;
Hothfield was my dwelling-place, and Christ is my salvation.
Now I am dead and in my grave, and all my bones are rotten.
When this you see, pray think of me, when I am quite forgotten.

The following epitaph is of a most remarkable nature. At *St. Peter's* Church in the East, *Oxford*, is a monumental inscription of a lady who died in child-birth, in the 62nd year of her age. It is under a brass affixed to a stone arch-monument against the wall in the north aisle of the church, whereon is the picture of a man and woman kneeling :—

Here lies the body of SIMON PARRET, M.A., late Fellow of Magdalen College, and ELIZABETH his wife, daughter of Edward Love, of *Aynho*, in the county of *Northampton*, Esqr., which Simon departed Sept. 24, 1584, in the year of his age 71. And Elizabeth departed in child-bed, December 24, 1572, in the year of her age 62.

We are not aware of having ever read a nobler termination to an epitaph to the memory of certain officers and privates who had perished in action. The inscription recited their names, and added, in touching solemn English phrase :—

Who died
Doing their Duty under the Flag
That Hangs over this Stone.

West Bradford (town), *Pennsylvania*. In this churchyard are seven tombstones, side by side, covering the remains of the Hon. NATHANIEL THURSTON and his six wives. They stand in order as follows : Mrs. BETSY THURSTON, died *November* 25, 1790, aged 34 ; Mrs. MARTHA THURSTON, died *May* 12, 1799, aged 32 ; Mrs. HULDAH THURSTON, died *September* 8, 1801, aged 24 ; Mrs. CLARISSA THURSTON, died *November* 14, 1803, aged 36 ; Mrs. MARTHA THURSTON, died *July* 30, 1804, aged 25 ; Mrs. MARY THURSTON, died *March* 3, 1808, aged 27 ; Hon. NATHANIEL THURSTON, died in *Lansinburgh*, *New York*, *October* 21, 1811, aged 56. MARTHA the second, it will be observed, was married and buried within nine months of the death of her predecessor, CLARISSA.

There is on the high north road, about a mile from *York*, a stone monument representing a woman upon her knees, with her hands clasped before her in a praying attitude. It is a memorial to the memory of URSULA SOUTHIEL, who married at the age of 24 (1512), one TOBY, a builder, at *Shipton*, a little village six miles to the north of *York* city. She was supposed to possess an uncommon penetration into futurity, and was so famous at the time of changing her maiden appellation that she derived the familiar cognomen of 'Mother Shipton!' The stone is now a shapeless mass, hardly a foot high, standing on a small triangular patch of ground. The original epitaph is said to have been :—

> Here lies one who never ly'd,
> Whose skill has oftentimes been tried.
> Her prophecies shall still survive,
> And ever keep her name alive.

On a stone in the wall of *Chiswick* Churchyard, *Middlesex* :—

This wall was made at ye charges of ye Right Honourable and trulie pious Lorde Francis Russell, Earl of Bedford, out of true zeale and care for ye keeping of this churchyard, and ye wardrobe of Godd's Saints, whose bodies lay therein buried, from violation by swine and other prophanation. So Witnesseth Wm. Walker, Vc., A.D. 1623.

On Lady MOLESWORTH, who was burnt to death by a

fire which broke out in her dwelling-house, *London*, 6th *May*, 1763 :—

> A peerless matron, pride of female life,
> In ev'ry state, as widow, maid, or wife,
> Who, wedded to threescore, preserved her fame—
> She lived a Phœnix, and expired in flame.

In *Camberwell* Church :—

Buried 5th *May*, 1658, ROSE, wife of WM. HATHAWAY, aged 103, who bore a son at the age of 63. Her husband, who was about the same age, survived her three years, and was buried 3rd *October*, 1661, aged 105.

Another :—

On ELIZABETH JONES who died 22nd November, 1775, aged 125.

Same church. There is an inscription in gold letters as follows: To the memory of NATHANIEL GODBOLD, Esqre, inventor and proprietor of that excellent medicine, the '*Vegetable Balsam*,' for the cure of consumptions and asthmas. He departed this life the 17th of *December*, 1799, aged 69 years.

In a church at *Carmarthen* :—

Here lyeth ye Body of ANNE, ye wife of JOHN PHILLIPS, of *Carmarthen*, Gent., born A.D. 1646, died *Feby*. ye 18th, 1720. She possessed in a great degree ye vertues and felicities of her sex, was ye mother of many children, of whom six survived her. She had ye uncommon happiness to see those six well settled and living all near her, in prosperous circumstances. The great duties of private life she discharged with equal prudence and success, and was at once an affectionate wife and a tender mother. She had ye comfortable satisfaction of seeing her six children married in ye same order they were born.

In *Esher* Church there is an inscription scarcely legible, which records of the mother of Mrs. MARY MORTON (who died *Ap*. 18, 1634) that she was 'the wonder of her sex and this age;' for she lived to see near four hundred issued from her loynes.

In the Churchyard of *Keyshoe*, in *Bedfordshire*, is the following inscription, now almost obliterated. The event to which it relates, together with the circumstances which are known to have been connected with it, appear too remarkable to be consigned to oblivion. No alteration has been admitted in copying the inscription from the stone, but in the spelling and grammar :—

In memory of the mighty hand of the Great God and Our Saviour Jesus Christ, who preserved the life of WILLIAM DICKENS, *April* 17th, 1718, when he was pointing the steeple, and fell from the ridge of the middle window in the spire, over the south-west pinnacle. He dropped upon the battlement, and there broke his leg and foot, and drove down two long coping stones, and so fell to the ground with his neck upon one standard of his chair, when the other end took the ground. He was heard by his brother to say, when near the ground, " Christ, have mercy upon me ! Lord Jesus Christ, help me !" It is added that he died *November* 29th, 1759, aged 73 years. The height from whence this person fell was not less than 132 feet, and his leg and foot were exceedingly fractured, but his injury in other respects was so trifling that he not only lived more than forty years afterwards, but within seven months from the time of his fall, he was capable of ascending the steeple a second time, and he then finished pointing the spire.

Conway, Carnarvonshire. On NICHOLAS HOOKES, Esq. :—

Here lieth the Body
Of NICHOLAS HOOKES, of *Conway*, Gentleman,
Who was the one-and-fortieth child of his Father,
William Hookes, Esq., by Alice his Wife,
And the Father of twenty-seven Children;
He died 20th of *March*, 1637.
This inscription was reviv'd in 1720, at the charge of
JOHN HOOKES, Esq.

Near *Dingwall* Church, *Rossshire*, is an obelisk rising in a pyramidal form, 57 feet high, being the burial-place of the family of Cromarty.

At *Litchfield, Conn.*, there is the following inscription on an old tombstone :—

Here lies the body of Mrs. MARY, wife of Dr. JOHN BUEL, Esq. She died *Nov.* 4, 1778, Ætat 90, having had 13 children, 101 grandchildren, 274 great-grandchildren, 22 great-great-grandchildren; total, 410; surviving, 336.

In the library of *Kirkby Lonsdale* Church, *Westmoreland*, is the following inscription :—

This library pulpit, and new loft, with the school-house,

were founded by HENRY WILSON, of Underby, who gave £1000 to the College, besides £35 yearly to seven poor scholars going to Queen's College, Oxford; to this Church and School £240, and to the poor of Kirkby Lonsdale lordship £500, besides many other gifts to pious uses in other places, by all of which he, being dead, yet speaks.

Epitaph :—

> The living know that they must die,
> But all the dead forgotten lie ;
> *Their memory and their sense is gone,*
> Alike unknowing and unknown.

On the death of his first son, by Ben Jonson :—

> Rest in soft peace, and ask'd, say here doth lie
> *Ben Jonson his best piece of poetry !*
> For whose sake, henceforth, all his verse be such,
> As what he loves may never like too much.

In *Peterborough* Cathedral are monuments to the memory of CATHARINE OF ARRAGON, wife of Henry VIII., and MARY QUEEN OF SCOTS, both of whom were buried here. The body of the latter was removed to *Westminster* Abbey.

Walton-on-Thames, Surrey. In the church at this place are preserved several brass plates, which were once laid over a grave-stone is evident, but in what part of the church is not known. One of these plates has a black-letter inscription to the memory of JOHN SELWYN, who is represented with his wife and eleven children in the attitude of prayer. And on another he is seated on the back of a stag, holding by one of the animal's horns with his left hand, and with his right plunging a sword into his neck. He was, it appears, under-keeper of the park at *Oatlands*, in the reign of Queen ; Elizabeth the bugle horn, the insignia of his office, is apparent in both figures. This man, according to tradition, which seems from the concurrent testimony of the plates to be well-founded, was extremely famous for his strength, agility, and skill in horsemanship, specimens of all which he exhibited in the park before the Queen at a grand stag-hunt. He in the heat of the chase suddenly leaped from his horse upon the back of the stag, both running at the same time with their utmost speed, and not only kept his seat gracefully, in spite of every effort of the affrighted beast, but drawing his sword, guided him with it towards the Queen, and when near her plunged it into his throat. Tradition says, the stag having, at the moment it was struck, thrown back its head, killed Selwyn by a blow of its horns. The epitaph is as follows: Here lieth ye bodye of JOHN SELWYN, Gentn., Keeper of her Majestie's Park of Otelande, under the Right Honourable Charles Howarde, Lord Admyral of Englande, his good lorde and master, who had issue by Susan his wyfe, V. sonnes and VI. daughters, all living at his death, and departed out of this worlde the XXII. day of March, A.D. 1587.

Westminster Abbey. On King HENRY V. :—

Here lies HENRY,
The Scourge of France,
1422.
Virtue surmounts all Opposition.
Here also,
With her Valiant Spouse, lies
The beautiful Catherine.
Keep from Sloth.

St. Martin's-in-the-Fields. On Sir EDWD. FANE :—

In memory of
Sir EDWARD FANE, Knt. of the Bath,
By Elizabeth, Relict of John Lord Darcey and Morwell.
He married Jane, third daughter of
Mr. James Stanier, Merchant of London.
Whom he left a sorrowful Widow.
He travelled five times into Spain,
Four times into Italy, thrice into France,
Twice into Turkey,
Where, at Aleppo, he resided six years,
And visited Jerusalem and the Holy Land,
Tripoli, Zidon, Acres, Joppa, Nazareth, Galilee,
The river Jordan, the Dead Sea, Bethlehem,
And other places :
And to show his undaunted Loyalty to
His Prince and Country,
He was a Volunteer in his Majesty's Fleet,
In the Three Days' Engagement against the Dutch in
1666,
And now,
After many Dangers passed, both by Sea and Land,
At the foot of this Pillar,
Lays down his Pilgrim's Staff,
In hopes of a heavenly Jerusalem,
In the 37th year of his age, Dec. 15, 1679.

In *Churchill* Church, *Somersetshire,* on a blue stone on the floor, are the figures of a man and woman, with eight children, in brass, with an inscription stating them to represent RALPH JENYNS, his wife JOANE, and their family, dated 1572. These brasses are in a beautiful state of preservation. He is habited as a knight in armour, with a curious head-piece, giving him a very singular appearance; above are three coats of arms.

The plague which prevailed in London, and unpeopled the village of *Eyam* in *Derbyshire*, is here strikingly exemplified. Six headstones and one tabular monumental stone yet remain to tell the tale of the total extinction of a whole family, with the exception of one boy, in the short space of eight days. The inscription, though much worn, was traceable in 1836, and may yet be so. The respective dates are :—

>   Elizabeth Hancock, died August 3, 1666.
>   John Hancock, sen.,   „   4, 1666.
>   John Hancock, jun.,   „   7, 1666.
>   Owen Hancock,   „   7, 1666.
>   William Hancock,   „   7, 1666.
>   Alice Hancock,   „   9, 1666.
>   Anne Hancock,   „ 10, 1666.

On the four sides of the tomb which contains the ashes of the father of this unhappy family of sufferers are the words, "*Horam Nescitis, Orate, Vigilate.*" A descendant of the boy mentioned above, whose preservation may almost be considered miraculous, introduced, about the middle of last century, into Sheffield, the method of plating ingots of copper with silver, and thus laid the foundation of one of the most lucrative manufactures of that town and its rival, Birmingham.

In *Aberlemno, Forfarshire*, are two obelisks which are

very fine pieces of antiquity, and were erected to commemorate the total defeat of the Danes by the Scots. They are about nine feet high, and covered with rude hieroglyphics.

In the year 1761, in the district of *Ben Ghisa*, in *Malta*, was discovered a sepulchral cave. In the wall of this cave was a hollow square, in which was cut, in Phœnician characters, the epitaph annexed, which Sir W. Drummond thus translated :—

> The Inner Chamber of the Sanctuary of the
> Sepulchre of Hannibal.
> Illustrious in the consummation of calamity,
> He was beloved.
> The people lament, when arrayed
> in order of battle,
> Hannibal the son of Bur-Melech.

In St. Mary's Churchyard, *Barnes, Surrey*, against the south wall, is fixed a small tablet of stone between two buttresses, to the memory of EDWARD ROSE, citizen of London, who died in July, 1653. The space between the buttresses is enclosed with wooden pales, and some rose trees are planted against the wall on each side of the tablet. This was done in pursuance of Mr. Rose's will, who left twenty pounds to the parish to be laid out in the purchase of an acre of land for the benefit of the poor, but out of the profits the churchwardens were to keep these pales in repair, to preserve the rose trees, and when they should decay to supply their place with others. All this has been very punctually complied with, the pales are in repair, the rose trees flourishing, and the parish

In *Weare* Church, *Somerset*, is an old brass plate, with an effigy, and the following inscription :—

>Of your charitie that passeth here by,
>Pray foe the soule of John Bedberie,
>That here doth lye,
>On whose soule Christ Jhu have mercie.

In All Saints' Church, *Kingston, Surrey*, on the brass-plate of a gravestone is the figure of a man habited in a gown with wide sleeves, which reaches to his feet, and the girdle studded with roses; his wife also standing beside him. The inscription beneath the figures is placed the wrong way upwards; but read from the bottom is as follows :—

>Roberti Cista Skerni corpus tenet ista
>Marmorie Petre Conjugis atque suæ,
>Qui validus, fidus, disertus, lege peritus,
>Nobilis, ingenuus, perfidiam renuit,
>Constans sermone, vita, sensu, ratione,
>Communiter cuique justitiam voluit,
>Regalis juris unicos promovit honores,
>Fallere vel falli res odiosa sibi,
>Gaudeat in celisqui vixit in orbe fidelis
>Nonas Aprilis pridie qui morit'
>Mille quadrigentis D'ni trigintaque septem
>Aim is ipsius Rex miserere Jesu.

Skern's wife is said to have been the daughter of the celebrated Alice Pierce, or Perrers, mistress of Edward III.

In St. Nicholas' Church, *Guildford, Surrey*, is a monument bearing the effigy of a priest habited in scarlet, with a dog at his feet, and an inscription whose date is in the 14th century. It is as follows :—" Hic jacet ARNALDUS BROCAS, Baculari......ut' usq, Iuris, Canonic' Lincoln' and Wellens', and qu'dam Rector isti' loci. qui obiit in Vig'la Assn' to's be'......Marie, Anno Domini, Millesimo, CCC. Nonagesimo quinto.

There is a curious relic of antiquity in the parish of *Rafford, Elginshire*, being a standing pillar near Forres, called "SWENOS STONE." Its height above ground is twenty-three feet, and about twelve or fifteen below, three feet ten inches broad, and one foot ten inches thick. On this stone, which is said to be the finest monument of the Gothic kind in Europe, are curiously carved a number of rude figures of animals, armed men, gigantic figures, and curious fret-work. It is supposed to have been erected in memory of the peace concluded between Malcolm and Canute, in 1012.

At *Killearn, Stirlingshire*, is a pyramid of white free-stone, nineteen feet square at the base, and a hundred and three feet high. It was erected in 1788, to the memory of George Buchannan, the celebrated poet and historian, who was a native of this place.

Near to the entrance of the town of *Newhaven, Sussex*, and close to the churchyard wall, stands an obelisk to commemorate the melancholy fate of his Majesty's ship "Brazen," Captain Hanson, which was wrecked here in *January*, 1800, and out of 105 persons one only escaped.

In *Campden* Churchyard, *Gloucestershire*, there are some ancient gravestones, one of the year 1386, and another 1401.

Epitaph, from a sheet entitled "A Crown a Crime; or, The Monarch Martyr," dated *Feb.*, 1648, in the British Museum :—

CHARLES I.

Behold the Mirror of a Prince pourtrayed,
The living Embleam of a glorious shade,
Whose Chair of State was late a scaffold made.

One, than whom never any did professe
More zeal to the Publique, and received lesse
Of more desert, and brought to more distresse.

That reall lustre to our Royal Garter,
That late inlarger of our Cities Charter,
Whose Crown the Crime that made this Monarch Martyr.

Adieu, Dear Prince, Death, like a loving friend
Hath crowned thy sufferings with a peacefull end,
While headless we our ruine must attend,

Nor can we lesse expect, Judgement's at hand
To scourge the follies of a sinfull Land,
What Brightman wrote we would not understand.

From the fatall period of a Charlemain,
Waine should a kingdom in her Charles—Waine,
But prayers nor tears might call him back again.

Lords should resigne their Patents to the Sword,
Lurdave should equall any English Lord,
O brave Platonick Levell! Martiall Boord.

Westminster Abbey :—

Æternæ memoriæ sacrum.

Sacred to the eternal memory of.

The name of the person, to whom immortality was thus secured, is almost obliterated ; and perhaps when alive he was little known, and as soon forgotten by the small circle of his friends and acquaintances.

In *Shiffnal* Church, *Shropshire*, are the following inscriptions :—

WILLIAM WAKELY was baptized at *Idsal*, otherwise *Shiffnal*, *May* the 1st, 1590, and was buried at *Adbaston*, *Nov.* 28, 1714. His age was 124 years and upwards; he lived in the reigns of eight kings and queens, D.P.

August 7th, 1776. MARY, the wife of JOSEPH YATES, of *Lizard Common*, within this parish, was buried, aged 127 years. She walked to London just after the fire in 1666, was hearty and strong 120 years, and married a third husband at ninety-two.

At *Bunbury, Cheshire,* a college was founded by Sir Hugh Calverley, about the year 1370. His tomb is still kept neat and clean, by a benefaction to the poor of the parish for that purpose, by Dame Mary Calverley, of *Lee*, in 1705.

In the Church of St. Buryan, *Cornwall*, is a coffin-shaped monument, inscribed " Clarice, la Cheffrie de Bolleit git icy. Dew de l'alme est mercy. Eke par l'alme punt, di ior de pardun averund." (Clarice, the wife of Geoffrey de Bolleit, lies here. God have mercy on her soul, and whoever prays for her soul shall obtain ten days' indulgence.)

St. Leonard's, Foster Lane, City. It was founded between 1231 and 1241. On the east end was engraven the name of JOHN BROKITWELL, the founder, and these rhymes :—

> Al yat wil gud warks wurch,
> Prey for yem that help thys church
> Geuuyng almys for Charite
> Pater noster, and Ave.

The following lines are more remarkable for quaintness of expression, than for their particular fitness for the character of one so bloodthirsty and infamous. Written for EADBURGA, the daughter of Offa, by his wife Quendrida, who married Bithric, or Bertric, King of the West Saxons (787) :—

> I was, I am not ; smiled, that since did weep ;
> Labour'd, that rest ; I waked, that now must sleep ;
> I play'd, I play not ; sung, that now am still ;
> Saw, that am blind ; I would, that have no will ;
> I fed that which feeds worms ; I stood, I fell ;
> I bade God save you, that now bid fareweil ;
> I felt, I feel not ; followed, was pursued ;
> I warr'd, have peace ; I conquer'd, am subdued ;
> I moved, want motion ; I was stiff, that bow
> Below the earth ; then something, nothing now ;
> I catch'd, am caught ; I travell'd, here I lie ;
> Lived in the world, that to the world now die.

Turning our thoughts from Eadburga, how pleasant it is to read of the good BERTHA, queen of King Ethelbert, of *Kent*, who contributed in no slight degree to the overthrow of the heathenism of the Saxons, and the sacred conversion of Britons to the Christian religion. She was buried in the porch of St. Martin's, *Canterbury*, and an Epitaph on her, now obliterated, but preserved by Leland, was to the following effect :—

Adorned with virtues, here lies the blessed Queen

Bertha, who was in favour with God, and greatly beloved by mankind.

On MARTIN LUTHER'S tomb :—

Judicio Pylium, genio Socratem, arte Maronem.

(In judgment a Nestor, in genius a Socrates, in art a Virgil.)

In the park of *Du Plessis*, near Senlis, is a handsome monument erected to the memory of CHRISTINE BOYER, wife of Luclan Buonaparte, Napoleon's second brother, on which is the following simple inscription :—

A daughter—wife—and mother—without reproach.

Willesborough Churchyard, near *Ashford*, in *Kent*. The following Epitaph (much defaced) was copied September 20th, 1764 :—

Here lieth entombed the body of WILLIAM MASTER, the second son of Michael Master, Esq. He living a Bachelor's Life, he came to an untimely Abel's death, at the age of 26 years, . . in his carriage—honest of his word, well respected and beloved of all. Elizabeth, the Daughter of John Hall, the Mother and Mourner for so great and incomparable a loss of so dear a Son . . . all memory—she hath erected this monument, with expectation of meeting in the Resurrection of Souls.—*Anno Domini*, 1634.

The preceding Epitaph relates to the unfortunate death of a young man, who was killed by his brother in a fit of jealousy, on account of an orphan young woman, who was protected by their father, and lived in his house. Mr.

Otway, happening to be on a visit to the neighbourhood soon after the unfortunate affair took place, learned the particulars, and made them the groundwork of his admirable tragedy, " *The Orphan.*"

On a tombstone in *Chiswick* Churchyard :—

J. Z. H. born *December* 19, 1802, died *January* 8, 1801.

By this it would appear that the child must have *died* rather less than twelve months *before* it was *born*.

In the parish of *Ahamlish, Sligo,* there is a burial-ground for drowned persons and unbaptized children ; and two burying-places, one for males and the other for females.

At St. Philip's, *Birmingham,* the following inscription expresses the opinion which was entertained of a remarkable dwarf :—

In memory of
MANNETTA STOCKER,
Who quitted this life the fourth day of May, 1819,
at the age of thirty-nine years.
The smallest woman of this kingdom, and one of the most accomplished.
She was no more than thirty-three inches high.
She was a native of Austria.

In the Church des Minimes, at *Luneville.* NICHOLAS FERRY, born November, 1741, at Plaisnes, in the principality of Salius, in the mountains called the Vosges, in the north-east of France. At the time of his birth was eighteen inches long, and weighed twelve ounces, and his height at the time of his death was thirty-three inches. The Duke of Lorraine (Stanislaus, King of Poland) felt his loss severely, and gave him a magnficient funeral. The heart of the dwarf was embalmed, and placed in a mausoleum erected to his memory. On this tomb his portrait was engraved, with an inscription in Latin. He was also modelled in wax, and the statue is still preserved in the cabinet of the Faculty of Medicine at Paris. The skeleton has been preserved among the anatomical collections of the Museum of Natural History in that city. The following is a translation of his epitaph :—

> Here lies
> NICHOLAS FERRY,
> A Lorraine,
> Nature's plaything. In virtue of the smallness of his stature, he was beloved by the modern
> Antoninus,
> Old in the flower of existence. For him five lustres were an age.
> He died the 9th of June, in the year 1764.

The famous ROBIN HOOD falling sick, was struck with remorse of conscience for his mis-spent life, and privately withdrew to a monastery in *Yorkshire*, where being bled by a monk he suffered himself to bleed to death. He died aged 42. The following is said to have been inscribed on the tombstone :—

> Underneath this cold marble stone,
> Through death's assault now lieth one,
> Known by the name of Robin Hood,
> Who was a thief and archer good.

Full twenty years or somewhat more,
He robb'd the rich to feed the poor ;
Therefore his grave bedew with tears,
And offer for his soul your prayers.

In the park near *Kirklees, Yorkshire,* was a monument to the memory of ROBIN HOOD, with this inscription :—

Here, undernead dis laid stean,
Lais Robert, Earl of Huntingtun ;
Nea arter az hie sa geud,
An pipl kauld him ROBIN HEUD,
Sich outlawz hi an iz men,
Vil England never si agen.

Obiit 24 Kal. Decembrio, 1247.

In the Baptist Churchyard at *Hoosick Falls, United States,* may be seen a rude board, which marks the grave of NAT SHIPMAN, the original of Fenimore Cooper's *Deerslayer,* in the well-known novel of that name, and of *Hawkeye* in " *The last of the Mohicans.*" There are documents to show, beyond doubt, the authenticity of this grave; and there is a movement on foot among the residents of Hoosick Falls to erect a monument worthy of a character immortalized in the romance of the northern wilderness. Until recently a son-in-law of the "Deerslayer," named Ryan, lived in Hoosick Falls.

At *Mortho, Devon,* Sir WILLIAM DE TRACY (one of the murderers of Thomas à Becket) built a church as a supposed expiation for his crime, and within the aisle his tomb still stands. An inscription in old Norman characters records the name and prayer of the dead :—

Syre WILLIAME DE TRACE. . . . Dieu de sa
alme eyt Mercy.

The Miller's tomb in *Sussex*. This curious monument is on *Heydown Hill*, near *Worthing*. It was erected in 1766, by JOHN OLIVER, the miller, 27 years previous to his disease, April 22, 1793, aged 84 years. The monument is strewed with many a pious text out of the burial service, and some poetical inscriptions—the effusion of his own muse. This singular man is said to have had his coffin for many years before his death; and that having a taste for mechanism, he caused it, upon touching a certain spring, to run on castors; it was wheeled every night under his bed. The summer-house near the tomb was also built by the miller; the delightful prospect from it constituted his greatest enjoyment. Oliver left twenty pounds per annum to keep this and the tomb from falling into decay.

In *Père-la-Chaise* Cemetery is the annexed inscription:—

Madame MILCENT,
Died March 10, 1824, aged 38 years.
Her death was accelerated by long sufferings,
Which she bore with great courage.
She carried in her body a child for eight years;
Twelve months living, and seven years dead.
To prove the truth of this, Doctors Dubois and
Bélivier extracted it at her decease, when it
was found to be well formed and
perfectly preserved.

It is now many years ago (1786) that the trial of STONEY BOWES took place. He married the Countess of Strathmore, whom he most cruelly tortured for years, but ultimately met the fate he deserved. The Countess obtained a divorce, and BOWES was ordered to pay a fine of £300 to his majesty; to be imprisoned in the King's Bench for three years; at the end of that time to find security for fourteen years, himself in £10,000 and two sureties of £5,000 each. The following epitaph will more clearly describe this brutal man :—

    Here rests
   Who never rested before,
   The most ambitious of men;
For he sought not virtue, wisdom, nor
Science; yet rose, by deep hypocrisy,
    By the folly of some,
    And the vice of others,
To honour, which nature had forbade,
And riches he wanted taste to enjoy.
   He saw no faults in himself,
   Nor any worth in others.
  He was the enemy of mankind;
   Deceitful to his friends,
  Ungrateful to his benefactors,
   Cringing to his superiors,
 And tyrannical to his dependants.
If interest obliged him to assist
Any fellow-creature, he regretted the
Effect, and thought every day lost
In which he made none wretched.
  His life was a continual series
   Of injuries to society,
  Disobedience to his Maker,
And he only lamented in despair
That he could offend them no longer.

> He rose by mean arts
> To unmerited honours,
> Which expire before himself.
> Passenger! examine thy heart,
> If in aught thou resemble him;
> And, if thou dost,
> Read, tremble, and reform;
> So shall he, who living
> Was the pest of society,
> When dead be, against his will,
> Once useful to mankind.

On the infamous FRANCIS CHARTRES, who died in 1731. He was *buried in Scotland*, and at his funeral the populace raised a riot, almost tore his body from the coffin, and threw dead dogs into the grave along with it. Dr. Arbuthnot wrote his epitaph:—

> Here continueth to rot
> The body of FRANCIS CHARTRES,
> Who, with an inflexible constancy,
> and
> Inimitable importunity of life,
> Persisted,
> In spite of age and infirmities,
> In the practice of every human vice,
> Excepting prodigality and hypocrisy:
> His insatiable avarice exempted him from the first,
> His matchless impudence from the second.
> Nor was he more singular,
> In the undeviating pravity of his manners,
> Than successful
> In accumulating wealth;

> For without trade or profession,
> Without trust of public money,
> And without bribe-worthy service,
> He acquired, or more properly created,
> A ministerial estate.
> He was the only person of his time,
> Who could cheat without the mask of honesty,
> Retain his primeval meanness
> When possessed of ten thousand a year;
> And having daily deserved the gibbet for what he did,
> Was at last condemned for what he could not do.
> Oh indignant reader!
> Think not his life useless to mankind:
> Providence connived at his execrable designs,
> To give to after ages
> A conspicuous proof and example,
> Of how small estimation is exorbitant
> Wealth
> In the sight of God,
> By His bestowing it on one of the most
> Unworthy of all
> Mortals.

In St. Salvador Church, *Fife*, is a most beautiful tomb of BISHOP KENNEDY, within which were discovered six magnificent maces, supposed to have been concealed in troublesome times. One of these was given to each of the Scottish universities, and three are preserved here.

In *Meigle* Churchyard, *Perthshire*, are the remains of the grand sepulchral monument of Vanora, said to have been the wife of Prince Arthur.

In a vault under the church at *Hythe, Kent,* is a remarkable pile of dry bones, twenty-eight feet long, and eight high, curiously arranged, and by the inscription, stated to be the remains of Danes and Britons killed in a battle near this place before the Norman Conquest.

It is said that Henry II., relying on the tradition of several ballads which recorded *Glastonbury, Somerset,* to be the burial-place of Arthur, ordered a search to be made, when a leaden cross was discovered, with a Latin inscription in rude Gothic characters, which were thus translated : Here lies the famous King Arthur, buried in the isle of *Avalow* (now, *Glastonbury*). Beneath was found a coffin hollowed out of the solid rock, wherein were the bones of a human body, supposed to be those of Arthur, which were afterwards deposited in the church, and covered with a sumptuous monument.

The chief monument in *Worcester* Cathedral is that of King John, standing in the midst of the choir ; on each side of which are those of the Bishops Wolstan and Oswald.

Christ Church, *Monmouth,* is noted for containing a sepulchral stone, on which is carved the figures of a man and woman, with their arms folded, standing on each side of a cross ; and a superstitious notion has prevailed that sick children have been miraculously cured by remaining all night in contact with some part of it, and it is related that in 1770, no less than sixteen were laid upon it.

In St. George's Chapel, *Windsor,* under the choir, are

the bodies of Henry VIII. and Jane Seymour, Charles I., and a daughter of Queen Anne. Adjoining the east end is a neat building erected by Henry VII., as a burial-place for himself and successors. A most sumptuous monument was afterwards erected here by Cardinal Wolsey, but he dying at Leicester, was there privately buried.

In the parish of *Kililagh, County Clare*, is a burial-ground called "Taumple-na-Spanig," or burial-place of the Spaniards. A considerable number of ships, which composed the celebrated Spanish Armada, were wrecked on this coast, and thrown with their crews on shore in this parish. The spot where they were buried has ever since borne the name of their nation.

There are in the choir of *Warwick* Church several handsome brass monuments of the ancient Earls of Warwick who are buried here, and one of the Earl of Essex, the unfortunate favourite of Queen Elizabeth.

On the north side of the church at *Kingston-on-Thames*, is a large stone on which tradition says the Saxon kings sat during their coronation, and by an inscription it appears that some of these kings were crowned in the market-place, and others in the chapel.

In *Alford* Church, *Kent*, is a handsome monument, 400 years old, to the memory of a Countess of Athol.

In the Market-place at *Devizes*, in *Wiltshire*, is a stone recording the Divine vengeance inflicted on an unhappy woman, who suddenly expired whilst in the act of imprecating the Divine curses on her own head, if she had not paid for some corn which she had purchased, though the money was afterwards found clutched in her hand.

In *Draycott* Churchyard, *Staffordshire*, may be seen one of the pyramidal stones with which the Danes are said to have marked the graves of their great men.

In the chancel of *Honington* Church, *Wiltshire*, is a black marble monument to the memory of G. STANLEY, Gent., who died 1719, aged 151.

At *Hatfield* Church, *Essex*, is a curious monument and cross-legged effigy to the memory of ROBERT VERE, the first Earl of Oxford, Lord High Chamberlain of England.

In the parish of *Cahircorney*, near *Limerick*, are the remains of the tomb of an ancient Irish outlaw, celebrated for his numerous robberies and musical compositions, named "Edmund of the Hill."

In *Keighley* Church, *Yorkshire*, is a very ancient tombstone which bears date 1023.

At *Festiniog, Merioneth*, are some stone monuments, called "Bedhew Gwyr Ardudwy," said to be the sepulchral monuments of some persons of note slain in battle between the men of Dyffryn Ardudwy and the men of Denbigh.

In the cathedral at *Icolmkill*, one of the *Hebrides*, are many curious tombs to the memory of the lords of the isles. Here also is an enclosed burying-ground containing the tombs of forty-eight Scottish kings, four kings of of Ireland, eight of Norway, and one of France, all buried here from the supposed sanctity of the ground.

There is a stone at *Bowes* Church, in *Yorkshire*, with an inscription on it to the Emperor Adrian. This stone was used in the beginning of the last century as a communion table.

In *Clynnog* Church, *Carnarvon*, is a tomb of St. Bueno, and resting on the tomb of this saint for one night was once held to be a certain cure for *all* diseases. The way of preparing the tomb was by covering it over with rushes, and the patients, after being washed in the neighbouring well, remained on it from night till morning.

In *Bridlington* Churchyard, *Yorkshire*, is a tombstone with this short inscription : 1542, THOMAS NEWMAN, aged 153.

There is an epitaph at *Copgrove* Church, *Yorkshire*, to JOHN WINCUPP, which states that he was rector 54 years ; was never concerned in any lawsuit ; was married 52 years, had six children all living ; and that he died in 1637, aged 86 years.

It appears from an ancient inscription in the churchyard of *Alford*, *Surrey*, that several Frenchmen took refuge from the massacre of St. Bartholomew, and set up a glass manufactory here.

At *Lamerton* Church, *Devon*, are the effigies of

Nicholas and Andrew Tremaine, twins, who were so like each other as scarcely to be distinguished. They were subject to the same pains, the same appetites, although at a considerable distance, and they were killed at Newhaven in 1663.

In *Llandaff* Church is a monument representing an emaciated corpse in a winding-sheet, in which the appearance of death, brought on by a long sickness, is admirably pourtrayed.

In the chancel of *Cheam* Church, *Surrey*, is a monument to the memory of LADY JANE LUMLEY, who died in 1577, and who translated the Iphigenia of Euripides and some of the orations of Isocrates into English, as well as one of the latter into Latin.

An old square tower stands in the churchyard of *Ardbraccan, Meath*, and the learned and indefatigable eastern traveller, BISHOP POCOCKE, was interred here in 1765.

At *Driffield, Yorkshire*, in 1784, a stone coffin was found, in which was a skeleton supposed to be the remains of Alfred the Great, there being in the chancel wall an inscription to that effect.

In *Eweline* Church, *Oxon*, is a curious monument of a former Duchess of Suffolk, with the Order of the Garter round her left arm.

In *Aberconway* Churchyard, *Carnarvon*, is an inscription on a tomb of one NICHOLAS HOCKER, importing that he was the one and fortieth child of his father, and had twenty-seven children himself.

Lanercost Priory, near *Naworth, Cumberland.* Its remains consist of the priory church, and some few of the offices of the monastery, fitted up for a farm-house. In the chancel, which is in ruins, amidst shrubs, brambles, and nettles, appear several very elegant tombs of the Dacre family. On a stone on the inside of the east wall is the following inscription :—ROBERT DE VALLIBUS, the son of Herbert, Lord of Gisland, founder of the priory of Lanercost, A.D. 1116.

By the side of the Abbey Church, *Paisley,* in a small vaulted chapel, is the monument of MARJERY BRUCE, daughter of King Robert Bruce, and near it are the graves of ELIZABETH MUIE and EPHEMIA ROSS, both consorts to Robert II.

On the east side of the portico of *Stepney* Church there is a stone with an inscription stating it to have been brought from the ruins of Carthage, and in the wall over the south portico is an ancient Saxon sculpture of the Crucifixion.

At *Monastesboyce* Abbey, *Louth, Ireland,* and west of one of the chapels, is a large stone cross with the name of MUREDOCH, King of Ireland, A.D. 520, still legible in large Irish characters. And in the ruin of one of the seven churches which once adorned *Glendalough, i.e.,* "The valley of the two lakes," in the county of *Wicklow,* is still shown a monument of the ancient Irish chieftain, O'TOOLE.

An inscription upon a tablet in a graveyard in *County*

Down, near *Belfast:* This is the grave of ——, wife of ——, who died on board the Scotia, May 24th, 1866, aged fifty-four. She died the death of the Christian, confessing the Son of God. Accept, O Ellen, the last honours I can pay thee. When living, thou wert much beloved by me. When dead, did I leave till I placed thee by the side of thy father? I David, love, do this. I will, Ellen, if prayer and gold can do it; for who can make an ocean grave? Farewell, my loved wife, though you have not left me, you have only first stepped into the lovely land of Jesus Christ, where we shall bid each other good morning, and sing together with my mother and thy mother, whom thou didst love with all thy great heart and mind, that new song we shall never weary to sing.

On the south side of the altar in *Tewkesbury* Church is a monument of delicate sculpture and beautiful proportions, in four stages of open arched work, with a tomb beneath, surrounded by an embattled border, and the sides ornamented alternately with double and single arches. On the tomb are the effigies of a knight and his lady. The former wears a round helmet, gorget, and hauberk of mail; at his feet is a lion, with a griffin's head for a crest. The lady has a dog at her feet, and appears in the square head-dress so commonly seen on tombs erected in the reign of Edward III.

Tradition assigns these figures to GEORGE, DUKE OF CLARENCE, brother to Edward IV., and his Duchess, ISABEL, who were both buried here; but it is not so, for neither the architectural decorations of the tomb, nor the dresses of the figures in any respect correspond with those of the latter part of the 15th century, but exactly resemble those of the reign of Edward III. Indeed, it appears that this splendid monument was erected to the memory of HUGH LE DESPENSER and ELIZABETH, who both died in the reign of Edward III.

Another splendid monument on the north side is enclosed by the sepulchral chapel founded by Isabel Countess of Warwick over the remains of RICHARD BEAUCHAMP, Earl of Worcester, her first husband, who was slain at the siege of Meaux, in France, in March, 1421.

A surcoat of arms long obscured authenticates an effigy, denominated by tradition "the king-making Earl of Warwick," to be that of EDMUND BARON DESPENSER, a hero on the field of Poictiers, who died in the year 1375.

The monuments to the abbots, as a matter of course, are numerous and exceedingly rich. In the south aisle is the tomb of ALANUS, the friend and biographer of Thomas à Becket, who died in the year 1202. In the south aisle of the nave, against the wall, is a monument of EDMUND BEAUFORT, the Duke of Somerset, beheaded after the battle of Tewkesbury.

The large blue slab shown as protecting the remains of the brave PRINCE EDWARD, so barbarously treated by his ruthless captors, retains no indications of its pretensions, its brasses having been removed; indeed, there is no authority for his having been buried in the spot. "His bodie," says Hollingshed, "was homelie interred with the other simple corpses." The probability is that he was thrown into one common grave with the other victims of the battle, who, on the Lancasterian side alone, numbered 3,000—as many as were slain at Waterloo, in this the age of gunpowder, rifles, and cannon.

At *St. Burians, Cornwall,* within the tower, on the pavement is an ancient tomb said to have been found, buried four feet, by the sexton while digging a grave. The inscription, in Norman-French, has been traced as follows : JANE, the wife of GEFFERY DE BOLAIT, lies here. Whosoever prays for her soul shall have five days' pardon.—M.LX.IX. But this appears to be incorrect. No date is mentioned, but the following may be taken as the translation : " Clarice, the wife of Geoffrey de Bolleit, lies here. God, of her soul have mercy. Who pray for her soul shall have ten days' pardon."

In the churchyard of *St. Madron,* in same county, is the often-quoted inscription on GEORGE DANIEL :—

> Belgia me birth, Britain me breeding gave,
> Cornwall a wife, ten children, and a grave.

Somewhat between the reverence of the old time and such doggrel as the above, is the monument in the church of St. Paul, to the memory of STEPHEN HUTCHENS, who died in 1709, leaving money for the repair of the church, and for dwellings for twelve poor persons in the parish. An allusion to the 112th Psalm informs the bystander that the said Stephen " saw his desire upon his enemies." The monument is in the Westminster Abbey style of that era, with representations of shattered vessels, warlike instruments, and trophies, with a profile of Queen Anne. The Cornish inscription above redeems the tomb from contempt :—

> Bounas heb dueth Eu poes Karens wei
> Tha Pobl Behodzhak Paull han Egles nei.

Which is thus translated :—

> Eternal life be his whose loving care
> Gave Paul an almshouse and the Church repair.

At *St. Martin's* Church, *Stamford, Lincolnshire* :—

In remembrance of that prodigy in nature, DANIEL LAMBERT, a native of *Leicester*, who was possessed of an excellent and convivial mind, and in personal greatness he had no competitor. He measured three feet one inch round the legs, nine feet four inches round the body, and weighed 52 stone 11 lb. He departed this life on the 21st of June, 1809, aged 39 years. As a testimony of respect this stone is erected by his friends in Leicester.

N.B.—The stone of 14 lb.

His coffin, consisting of 112 superficial feet of elm, was rolled upon two axletrees to the grave.

On the tombstone of JAMES WEIR, in the parish of *Carluke, Scotland*, is the following inscription :—

This child, when only 13 months old, measured three feet four inches in height, 39 inches round the thigh, and weighed five stone. He was pronounced by the faculties of Edinburgh and Glasgow to be the most extraordinary child of his age upon record.

In the old churchyard at *Leith* an inscription denotes the resting-place of ELLEN NEILSON, spouse of Thomas

Gladstone, merchant, in *Leith*, who died July 17th, 1800, aged 66 years ; and of THOMAS GLADSTONE, husband of Ellen, who died the 11th of May, 1809, aged 76 years. Thomas Gladstone, who is thus commemorated, was a prosperous trader in Leith. By his marriage with Ellen, daughter of Walter Neilson, of Springfield, he became father of Sir John Gladstone, Baronet, of Fasque, who was born at Leith on the 11th of December, 1764. Sir John's fourth son, the Right Honourable William Ewart Gladstone, after a distinguished career as a statesman, obtained the Premiership in 1868.

In *Hammersmith* Church is a monument of black and white marble, above which is a bust of CHARLES I., beneath this inscription :—

<blockquote>
This effigy was
erected by the special appointment of
Sir Nicholas Crispe, Knight and Baronet,
as a grateful commemoration of that
glorious martyr, King CHARLES
the First, of blessed
memory.
</blockquote>

Beneath is an urn, and on the pedestal that supports it are these lines :—

Within this urn is entombed the heart of Sir NICHOLAS CRISPE, Knight and Baronet, a loyal sharer in the sufferings of his late and present Majesty. He first settled in the trade of gold from Guinea, and there built the castle of Cormantine. Died the 26th of *February*, 1665, aged 67 years.

The body of Sir Nicholas lies in *St. Mildred's, Bread Street.* He was the founder of Brandenburgh House; improved the arts of paper-making, powder-making, and brick-making; gave £700 towards the building of Hammersmith Church, besides beautifying the building, and his charities to the poor were equal to his bounties in other directions.

INDEX

TO EPITAPHS AND OBSEQUIES.

	PAGE
Abraham	8
Abbott, Mordecai	66
Actors, On	135, 136, 141, 142
Adam	2
Adams, John	108
Adams, Julia	181
Adrian, Emperor	230
Ælinum	1
Æschylus	125
Aftrid	203
Alanus	234
Aldersey, Harriet	50
Aldersey, Wm.	50
Aldridge, Thomas	183
Alexander, Mary	45
Alfred the Great	231
Alston, Ned	178
Aleppo	9
Anacyndaraxes	103
Anglesea, Leg of Marquis of	197

INDEX.

	PAGE
Ann, Queen	228, 235
Antrum, Johannes	66
Arabia	4, 9, 13
Aragon, Catherine of	209
Architects, On	91
Aretin, Peter	99
Argyle, Marquis of	54
Arthur, King	227
Arthur, Prince	7, 226
Ashford, Mary	76
Asia	5, 8, 9
Astrologer, On an	105
Athenians	2, 5
Athol, Countess of	228
Author, On an	104
Bachelor, On a	156
Bacon, W.	76
Bactrians	5
Bagshaw, Edward and Margaret	69
Baker, On a	96
Balearians	7
Bancroft, Archbishop	147
Banwell	15
Barber, On a	101
Barber, John	139
Barford, Susanna	168
Barham, James	103
Barker, Cornelius	91
Basset, Richard	159
Batchelor, Nell	108
Battay, Sarah	181
Beauchamp, Richard	234
Beaufort, Edmond	234
Beaufort, Mr.	203

	PAGE
Beautiful Epitaphs	22
Becket, Thomas à	222, 234
Bedberie, John	214
Bedford, Duke of	205
Bee, Cornelius	14
Beggar, On a Cornish	108
Beighton, Rev.	,132
Belivier, Dr.	223
Bell Founder, On a	93
Bellows Maker, On a	90
Bell Ringer, On a	103
Ben Honest	122
Bent, Jane	174
Bertha, Queen	218
Beuno, St.	230
Bithrie or Bertrie, King	218
Blackadder, Rev. J.	54
Blacket, Joseph	92
Blacksmith, On a	88, 89
Blenner, Haysell, Lieut.-Col.	65
Bloomfield, Robert	143
Blundon	15
Boardman, R.	75
Boat, Judge	
Bodger, Samuel	123
Bolait, Jane	235
Bolait, Gefferyde	235
Bolleit, Clarice	217
Bond, Thomas and Wife	161
Bonney, Rev. H. K.	143
Boo, Prince Lee	46
Bourne, Nehemiah	63
Bowen, Matilda	77
Bowes, Stoney	223
Bowles, Rev. W. L.	3

INDEX.

	PAGE
Box, Mr.	155
Boxer, Master Thomas	164
Boyer, Christine	219
Brain, O'Teague	166
Brassgirdle, J.	77
Brawne	108
Brewer, On a	93
Brickmaker, On a	95
Bridgewater, Joseph	32
Bridgewater, Hannah and Elizabeth	32
Britons	7
Brittany	15
Brocas, A.	214
Brockitwell, John	218
Brougham, Lord	95
Bruce, King Robert	232
Bruce, Margery	232
Brown, Maria	177
Buchan, Earl of	138
Buchannan, George	215
Buel, Dr. John	208
Buel, Mrs. Mary	208
Builder, On a	91
Bullen, Rev. H.	111
Bunn, John	144
Buonaparte, Lucien	219
Burgoin, William	113
Burke, Richard	186
Burmese	10
Bur-Melech	213
Burns, Robert	55, 106, 185
Bushy, Thomas	46
Butler, Samuel	139, 140
Button, Richard	173
Byng, Admiral	121

	PAGE
Byron, Lord	56, 92, 141, 159, 199
Cabzll, Robert	15
Cadman, John	184
Caligula	5
Calverley, Sir Hugh	217
Cambricusis, Giraldus	7
Camden	14
Cameron, Dr.	117
Campbell, Lord	15
Canute	215
Card Maker, On a	94
Carpenter, On a	167
Carter, R.	171
Carthew, Joan	193
Carrie	23
Carrier, On a	108
Catherine, Queen	210
Caves, T.	196
Caxton, William	86
Cecill, Lady	43
Chad	15
Chairman, On an Irish	156
Chaldeans	5
Chambers, Ephraim	176
Chard, Dr.	114
Charles, I.	202, 216, 228, 237
Charles II.	126
Charlton, John	98
Chartres, Francis	225
Cherriman, George	47
Cheshyre, Robert	27
Chest, Rev.	194
Chinese	8—10
Circassians	12

	PAGE
Clarence, Duke of	233
Clay, Cecil	109
Clergymen, On	128, 129, 130, 131, 132, 133
Clifford, Lord	203
Cnidius, Clefias,	3
Coachman, On a	111
Coach Proprietor, On a	101
Cobblers, On	92
Cobbold, Marian E.	84
Cobham, Lord	197
Colchians	6
Coleridge, S. T.	140
Coles, Rev. W.	129
Colman, George	192
Collyer, Rev. A.	66
Colnett, Rev.	131
Combs, John O.	146
Comedians, On	134, 135
Congoese	11
Cook, On a	99, 107
Cook, T.	29
Cooper, Fenimore	222
Coram, Captain Thomas	28
Corbett, Sir U.	43
Cormack, A. Mac	55
Cornish Beggar, On a	108
Coroner, On a	112
Coster, Claude	196
Cotton, J.	131
Covenanters, On the	53
Cowper, W.	156
Crabtree, Thomas	176
Cricketers, On	103
Crisp, Sir Nicholas	237
Crouch, R.	174

	PAGE
Croker, S. P.	22
Cromarty	208
Crossfield, Dr.	117
Crowley, Sir Ambrose	99
Cruikshanks, Rev. J.	55
Crumbleholme, Samuel	14
Crytoft, Robert	177
Cullum, Sarah	73
Curtis, William	35
Curtis, Sir W.	191
Dacre	232
Dalziel, T.	55
Daniel, George	235
Darcey and Merwell, Lord	211
Davis, Rev. George	128
Death, Mr. and Mrs.	184
Dent, John	72
Despenser, Hugh Le and Wife	234
Devonshire, Duke of	107, 157
Dibdin, Thomas	189
Dickie, Molly	155
Dickens, William	207
Dickonson, John	74
Digby, Lady	41
Digby, Lord	41
Doctors, On	113, 114, 115, 116, 117
Dog, On a	198
Downie, Macom	165
Drake, John	176
Draper, On a	104
Drummond, Sir W.	213
Dryden, John	37
Dubellay	120
Dubois, Dr.	223

	PAGE
Duck, S.	134
Dudley, Joseph and Walter	157, 180
Dudley, M.	157
Dugdale, Sir W.	137, 138
Dunch, Captain J.	118
D'Urfey, Tom	152
Dustman, On a	112
Duval	203
Dyer, On a	93, 94
Eadburga	218
Eater, On a great	194
Edward III.	214, 233, 234
,, IV.	202, 233
,, V.	202
,, VI.	202
Edward, Prince	234
Egypt	4, 5, 9
Eldred, Charles	80
Elizabeth, Queen	202, 210, 228
Elizabeth, Princess	202
Elphinstone, James	24
Engineer, On an	85, 95, 96
England	4—7
Epitaphs on a Wife	28, 48
,, on a Young Lady	23, 32, 33, 34, 36, 51
,, on Infants	33, 38, 44, 59, 73, 75, 81, 82, 153, 171
,, on Three Children	36, 58, 193
,, on Martyrs of Covenant	53
,, on a Friend	55, 57
,, on a Family	24
,, Beautiful	22
,, Miscellaneous	201
Essex, Earl of	228
Estelle	24

	PAGE
Ethelbert	218
Ethiopians	3—9
Euphorion	125
Eve	3
Fairclough, Richard	61
Fairfax, Sir Thomas	127
Fane, Sir Edward	211
Faux, Guy	201
Fenton, Elijah	43
Ferguson, John	120
Ferry, Nicholas	220
Fido, Signor	198
Fidoe, Rev. A.	72
Fifer, On a	183
Fish, Mr.	171
Flavel, Thomas	48
Fletcher, Miss	14
Fletcher, Thomas	124
Floyer, Mrs. A.	26
Foche, Elizabeth	60
Fontaine	87
Fox, H.	89
Foxhounds, On Master of	98
Foote, Samuel	135, 148
Frank and Betty	165
Franklin	86
Franklin, Benjamin	87
Freeland, Mrs. Rebecca	163
French	2, 9, 13
Freer, Nathaniel	147
Game, John	60
Gammon, Rev. J.	67
Garrick, David	141, 142
Gaunt, John of	202

	PAGE
Gay, John	51, 139
Gedge, L.	87
Genevra	7
Gee, Ellen	179
Geographer, On a	103
George III.	149
Georgian	12
German	9
Giraldus Cambriensis	7
Gladstone, T. and J. B. and W. E.	237
Godbold, Nathaniel	206
Godfrey, Dr.	114
Godfrey, Sir Edmund Bury	101
Goldsmith, Oliver	142
Goldsmith, On a	92
Gore, Dame Elizabeth	40
Gore, Sir W.	40
Gray, Katherine	98
Gregory, Pope	7
Griffiths, George	125
Greenfat, Sir Humphrey	99
Greek	2, 5, 13
Greentree, J.	159
Greyhound, On a	198
Griffith, Jane	34
Griffiths, George	125
Grim, Mulciber	8
Grocer, On a	106
Grose, Francis	148
Grotesque Epitaphs	144
Gryphe	87
Guinea	11
Guise, Sir John	160
Gunter, James	26
Guthrie, Mr.	54

	PAGE
Guy Faux	201
Guy, Thomas	39
Gwynn, Martha	172
Hall, Elizabeth	106
Hall, John	106
Hall, Randle	202
Hall, Mrs. Susannah	137
Hancock, The Family of	212
Hannibal	213
Hanson, Captain	215
Harckness, J.	58
Harper, Roger and Wife	106
Harsnett, Archbishop	131
Haselton, Mary	78
Hathaway, Rose	206
Hatherleigh	13
Hawke, Lord	119
Hayley	89
Haysell, Lieut.-Col. W. B.	65
Heiwood, Peter	201
Henry II.	7, 203, 227
,, IV.	202
,, V.	210
,, VII.	141, 202, 228
,, VIII.	141, 202, 209, 228
Hen-pecked Squire, On a	194
Herbert, of Gisland	232
Hermit, On a	149
Herodotus	3
Herrick	137, 141
Heruli	6
Hewlin, W.	105
Hexham	13
Highwayman, On a	178

INDEX.

	PAGE
Higley, John	166
Hill, Captain	120
Hill, George	152
Hill, John	31, 153
Hindoo	12
Hippisley, John	135
Hiseland, William	126
Hitchin, Jane	173
Hocker, Nicholas	231
Hodgkins, Maria	81
Hogarth, William	135
Holme, Rev. B.	70
Holmes, Thomas	67
Hollingshed	234
Hollingshed, Matthew	158
Holy Willie, On	186
Honeywood, Rev. M.	132
Hood, Robin	221
Hook, Nathaniel	14
Hookes, J.	208
Hookes, Nicholas	208
Hookes, W.	208
Horwood, Miss	14
Hottentot	11
Hough, Thomas	202
Hough, Dr.	14
Houlden	101
Hubble, Richard	39
Huddlestone, John	175
Hughes, Ann	149
Humbrick, Jeems	164
Huntingdon, Earl of	222
Huntsman, On a	110
Hutchens, Stephen	235
Huxley, John	194

	PAGE
Ichthyophagi	6
Ilger, Rev. John	132
India	4, 12
Ireland	4—13
Irish Chairman, On an	156
Isaac	3—8
Isabel, Duchess	233
Isnell, Peter	100
Ivalsir	203
Jackson, John	155
Jackson, George	176
James, Elias	137
James I.	202
James, John	107
Jeffrey, Daniel	182
Jews	2
Jenyns, Ralph and Wife	211
Jenyngs, Soame	107
Jerusalem	14
John, King	227
Johnson, Mrs. Ann	69
Johnson, Dr.	107
Jonson, Ben	137, 141, 209
Jones, Elizabeth	206
Jones, Captain	195
Jones, Joseph	189
Jones, William	164
Jortin	24
Joseph	3
Keeling, William	121
Kemp, Thomas	187
Kemp, Robert	153
Kendrick, Richard	187
Kennedy, Bishop	226

INDEX.

	PAGE
Kenwick, James	54
Kiffin, William	105
Kildare, Earl of	156
Knox, John	54
Knollys, Mrs. Ann	71
Lacedemonians	2
Lambe, Edward	112
Lambert, Daniel	236
Landor, W. S.	140
Laplander	12
Latimer, Nicholas	61
Laurie, J.	186
Lawyer, On a	109, 110
Leah	3
Lee, John	154
Lee, Mrs.	190
Lee, Tom	190
Leg, On a	197
Leland	218
Letter Founder, On a	90
Lewars, Jessey	56
Lewes, Jonathan	81
Lewis, Bryant	35
Libyan	4
Lightfoot, Bernard	177
Lilliard, Maiden	195
Lilly, W.	105
Lillywhite	103
Linnæus	105
Linen Draper, On a	104
Linus	1
Lisle, Sir George	127
Little Jemmy	167
Lockhart, J. G.	109

	PAGE
Long, Miss	172
Love, Edward	204
Looney, Lady O'	148
Lorraine, Duke of	221
Lucas, Sir Charles	127
Lumber, Hugh	33
Lumley, Lady Jane	231
Luther, Martin	219
Lyttleton, Lucy	23
Malmsbury, William of	15
Manning, Rev. O.	130
McFee, J. and Wife	187
Maginn, W.	109
Magistrate, On a	109
Marr, Mrs. Celia	80
Marr, Timothy	80
Martyr, On a	130
Mary, Queen	202
Master, Rob	96
Master, William	219
Maton, J. and A.	79
Mauleverer, Sir Thomas	57
Maurice, Annie C.	47
Mayor, Lord, On a	104
Meekie	106
Mercy	125
Messer, Tammy	90
Menestrier, Jean Le	175
Meynell, Mary	59
Middleburgh	31
Middleditch, William	123
Millicent, Madame	223
Miller, Joe	134
Mills, John	110

	PAGE
Miltiades	125
Mingrelians	12
Minors, Captain W.	118
Miscellaneous Epitaphs	201
Misers, On	146 147,
Molesworth, Lady	205
Molesworth, Viscount and Wife	25
Monmouth, Duke of	105
More	145, 187
More, Hannah	35
Moore, Robert and Wife	172
Morgan, Edward	202
Morrison W.	26
Morrison, Janet	26
Morton, Mrs. Mary	207
Morton, Roger	194
Moses	8
Mounsey, Dr.	116
Mudd, Matthew	173
Muddeford, Sir John	201
Muie, Elizabeth	232
Muredock, King	232
Napoleon	219
Naturalist, On a	105
Neilson, E. and W.	236
Newfoundland Dog, On a	199
Newman, Thomas	230
None	146
Nootka Sound	12
Northamptonshire	16
Obsequies, Remarks on	1
Offa	218
Okey, Samuel	

	PAGE
Old Maid, On an	154
Oliver, John	223
Oonalaska	12
Ooden, Betsey	167
Orator, Stump	156
Oswald, Bishop	227
O'Toole	232
Otheite	12
Otway, Thomas	220
Oxford, Earl of	229
Pacific Islanders	9
Pady, James	95
Painter, On a	135
Palfreyman, J.	170
Palmerston, Lord	36
Parish Clerk, On a	99, 100
Parker	111
Parker, Admiral	56
Parker, Miss	56
Park-keeper, On a	107
Parkins, Thomas	102
Partridge, J.	116
Parr, Thomas	202
Parret, S. and Wife	204
Paston, Mrs. M.	37
Passingham, Richard	31
Pauper, On a	153, 163
Pearce, Dickey	180
Peck, Mr.	195
Pedestrian, On a	192
Pembruge, Catherine	30
Pembruge, W.	30
Penton, Rev. S.	129
Pennyman, John	62

INDEX.

	PAGE
Percival, Jane	62
Periwinkles, On a Crier of	110
Persian	3—6
Perrers, Alice	214
Peter, Alexander	99
Phillips, Anne	206
Philpots, Richard	166
Philosopher, On a	102
Physician, On a	114, 116
Pickering, Sophia O.	79
Pie-Woman, On a	108
Pig, On a	200
Pin Maker, On a	96
Plessis, Cardwell	131
Pococke, Bishop	231
Poet Laureate, On a	141
Poets, On	136
Pomponazzi	102
Pope, Alexander	43
Pope, Dr. Walter	116
Portmans, Elizabeth	65
Pottery Shop, On a Keeper of a	98
Powell, Vavasor	71
Prestwich, Sir John	203
Prichard, Dr.	14
Prichard, R. and Wife	188
Pride, Walter	93
Prince of Wales, Frederick	149
Printers, On	86, 87
Proctor, Thomas	172
Professional Epitaphs	85
Prynne, William	110
Ptolemy	6
Publican, On a	93, 189
Punster, On a	188

	PAGE
Purdue, Thomas	93
Puzzling Epitaphs 87, 112, 114, 136, 151, 158 160, 183, 196,	
Quack, On a	111
Quarrelsome Man, On a	191
Quendrida	218
Quick, William	171
Quin, James	141
Raid, Frank	100
Rainsborough, Col. Thos.	124
Ramsay, Allan	141
Randall, J.	187
Rand, Ned	191
Rebecca	3
Reed, Isaac	189
Remant, S.	157
Reson, Ellen	151
Richard II.	202
Richelieu, Cardinal	131
Richmond, Leigh	44
Rigg, J. and A.	74
Robert II.	232
Robin Hood	221
Robinson, W. S. and A.	83
Romans	2, 5, 8, 13
Roper, Henry	160
Rosamond, Fair	203
Rose, Edward	213
Rose, Hugh	51
Rose, Miss	51
Ross, Ephemia	232
Ross, John	165
Round, John	173
Routleigh, George	94

	PAGE
Royston, Sarah	31
Ruling Elder, On a	180
Rumbold, S.	192
Rupack, Abba Thulla	46
Russell, Lord	205
Russian	10
Ryan	222
Sailors, On	118, 119, 120, 121, 122
Sapper, Thomas	174
Sarah	8
Sarai	3
Sardanapalus	103
Satirist, On a	140
Saxons	9
Saul, Daniel	89
Scarron	142
Schoolmaster, On a	106
Scolding Woman, On a	190
Scot, Col. Thomas	57
Scot, Grace	57
Scotland	4
Scots, Mary Queen of	209
Scott, John	93
Scott, Margery	177
Scott, Maria	78
Scythians	6
Sellars, Ann	169
Sellars, Isaac	169
Selwyn, John	209
Serle, W.	45
Sexton, On a	189
Sexton, S.	145
Seymour, Jane	228
Shakspeare, William	136, 137, 138, 146

	PAGE
Sharpless, Will	96
Shaw, John	188
Sheepstealer, On a	187
Shenstone, William	142
Shipman, Nat	222
Shipton, Mother	205
Shoemaker, On a	92
Shorthose, Tom	155
Shute, Amos	173
Silo, Prince	158
Sise	160
Skelton, Joseph	141
Skern and Wife	214
Skinner, Rev. J.	42
Skypwith, Richard	49
Smith, Francis	63
Smith, Isaac	123
Smith, John	14
Smith, Lucian	63
Smyth, Henry	97
Smollett, Dr. Tobias George	117
Smuggler, On a	188
Snell, Martha	184
Soldiers, On	122, 123, 124, 125, 126, 127
Solicitor, On a	151
Somerset, Duke of	234
Somewille, W.	33
Southiel, Ursula	205
Spalding, Joseph	122
Sparks, Charlotte	203
Spartans	8
Speid, Alexander	193
Spencer, Earl	86
Stafford, Dr.	117
Stainer, James	211

	PAGE
Stanley, G.	229
Stanley, Sir Thomas	138
Stanislaus, King of Poland	221
Statesman, On a	106
Stephenson, Joseph	25
Stewart	38
Steele, Mrs.	22
Steele, Pat	163
Stiller, Peter	173
Stocker, Mannetta	220
Stokes, S.	144
Stone	145
Stone, Captain	191
Strabo	103
Strange, Mr.	110
Strathmore, Countess of	223
Strozzi, Leon	120
Style, Lieut.-Col. W.	70
Suffolk, Duchess of	231
Suffolk, Earl of	180
Swannell, James and Harriet	59
Swift, Dean	156
Swinburne, Martha	52
Swithin, St.	15
Sydney, Sir Philip	112
Sykes, John	167
Syl	90
Sylvester, Mrs. H.	68
Sylla, Cornelius	5
Symons, William	170
Tailor, On a	100, 101
Tartars	12
Tayler, Rev. Robert	133
Taylor, Dr. Rowland	130

Teetotaller, On a	191
Thomas, Mary	68
Thompson, James	138
Thucydides	3
Thurston, Nat and six Wives	204
Thurulf	203
Thwaites, F.	82
Tiberius, Emperor	5
Tibullus	141
Tiffey, Jack	188
Timocreon	152
Tonquinese	11
Tonson, Jacob	86
Tracy, Sir W. de	222
Trade Epitaphs	83
Transposing Epitaph	158
Traps, Robert	92
Tremaine, Andrew	231
Tremaine, Nicholas	231
Trivulcuis	152
Trollope, Robert	91
Tucker, Edward	70
Turberville, Dr. D'Aubigny	115
Turks	9—11
Turville, Judy	31
Two Lovers, On	153
Tyler, Wat	102
Tyrer, Rev. R.	75
Undertaker, On an	96
Underwood, Captain	171
Vallibus, R. de	232
Vanbrugh, Sir John	91
Vanora	226

	PAGE
Vere, Robert	229
Vernon, Thomas	172
Verheyen, P.	113
Virgil	141
Wake, Mr.	99
Wakely, W.	217
Wales, Prince of	149
Walker, John	85
Wall, Randall	202
Wallis, Robert	90
Walton, Henry	106
Walworth, Sir W.	102
Wang, Henry	148
Warner, John	104
Warwick, Earl and Countess of	228, 234
Watchmaker, On a	94
Waterhouse, Rev. J.	128
Watt, James	95
Weaver, On a	89, 90
Webb, Frederick	101
Weir, James	236
Wells, Dr.	14
West, Ann	182
West, Gilbert	38
Westley, S.	140
Whitehead, Paul	140
Wicker, William	47
Wilson, Bishop	133
Wilson, Captain	46
Wilson, Henry	209
Wilson, William	188
William III.	116
Williams, David	159
Williams, Sir C. Hanbury	29

	PAGE
Williams, William	32
Willing, W.	176
Willis, Caroline	25
Willis, H. N.	25
Wincupp, John	230
Witty Epitaphs	144
Wix, William	169
Wolsey, Cardinal	228
Wonderful Epitaph	158
Woodcock, Sir Thomas	155
Woodcock, William	166
Woodier, Mrs.	152
Woodman, On a	104
Woollett, William	102
Woolstan, Bishop	227
Worcester, Bishop of	41
Worcester, Earl of	234
Worlidge, Thomas	90
Worsdale, James	172
Wraxall, Sir Nathaniel	192
Wren, Sir Christopher	91
Wrestler, On a	102
Wright, Hugh	160
Wright, Margaret	160
Wright, Thomas	25
Wylde, Miss	35
Wylde, Rev. H.	35
Wynter, Sir Edward	126
Yates, Mary	217
Young, Miss A.	153

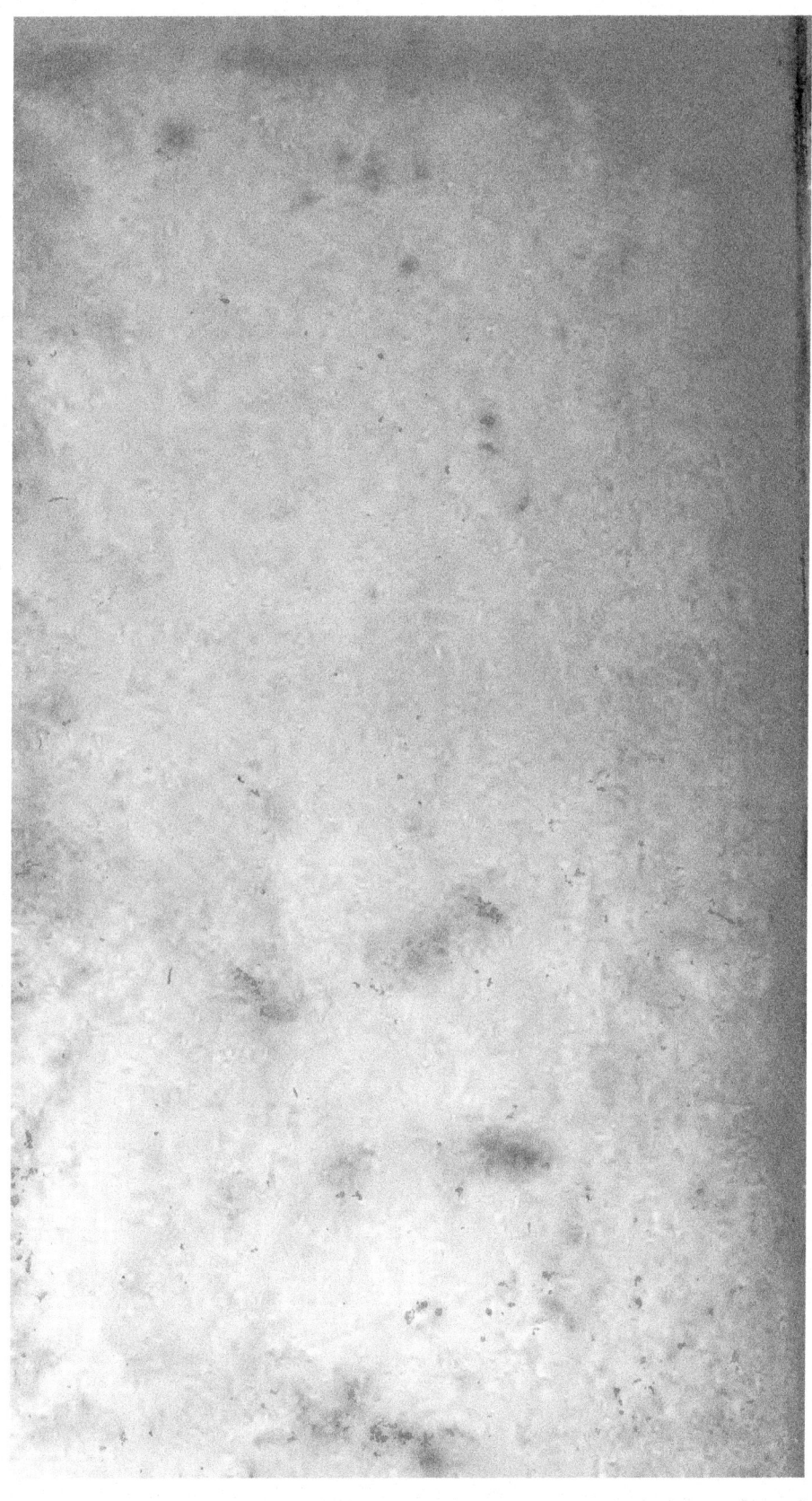

ImTheStory.com

Personalized Classic Books in many genre's

Unique gift for kids, partners, friends, colleagues

Customize:
- Character Names
- Upload your own front/back cover images (optional)
- Inscribe a personal message/dedication on the inside page (optional)

Customize many titles Including
- Alice in Wonderland
- Romeo and Juliet
- The Wizard of Oz
- A Christmas Carol
- Dracula
- Dr. Jekyll & Mr. Hyde
- And more...

CPSIA information can be obtained
at www.ICGtesting.com
Printed in the USA
BVOW06s1010130117
473440BV00010B/70/P